MURDER TIMES SIX

MURDER TIMES SIX

THE TRUE STORY OF THE WELLS GRAY PARK MURDERS

ALAN R. WARREN

COPYRIGHT

MURDER TIMES SIX: The True Story of the Wells Gray Park Murders
Written by Alan R. Warren

Copyright @ 2020 by Alan R. Warren

All rights reserved. No part of this book may be reproduced, scanned, or distributed in any printed or electronic form without permission of the author. The unauthorized reproduction of a copyrighted work is illegal. Criminal copyright infringement, including infringement without monetary gain, is investigated by the FBI and is punishable by fines and federal imprisonment. Please do not participate in or encourage privacy of copyrighted materials in violation of the author's rights. Purchase only authorized editions. This is a work of nonfiction. No names have been changed, no characters invented, no events fabricated.

Cover design, formatting, layout, and editing by Evening Sky Publishing Services

Published in United States of America

CONTENTS

Foreword   vii
Preface   xiii

PART I

1. Never Forget Her Eyes   3
2. Far Away From Home   10
3. It's All Decided For Us   15
4. I Promise To Try   22
5. Night Comes Down   27
6. The Waiting Seems Like Eternity   32
7. No Place Left To Hide   40
8. Eyes of a Stranger   54
9. I'm a Danger To Myself   64

PART II

10. A Crack In My Soul   77
11. Sleeping With the Enemy   113
12. My Pain's Not Ashamed To Repeat Itself   122
13. Freedom Comes When You Learn To Let Go   128
14. Forensic Optography   149
15. Fight From the Inside   153
16. There's No Place For Us   176

17.	Man On The Prowl	193
18.	Once a Pedophile, Always a Pedophile?	205
19.	Parole For Killers In Canada	214

PART III

20.	Johnson Bentley Aquatic Centre	231
21.	50th Wedding Anniversary	236
22.	Janet & Karen Johnson	238
23.	The Unbelievable Swede by JACKIE JOHNSON	242
24.	John Gorman 65th Birthday Letter by BOB JOHNSON	247

Afterword	253
Acknowledgments	257
References	263
About the Author	269
Also By Alan R. Warren	271

FOREWORD

Ron German, Sgt. RCMP (retired)

Helping solve a mass murder is not commonplace in policing careers. Fortunately, such ghastly and incomprehensible events seldom occur. I, however, was one of those who found myself face to face with a mass murderer. At first, I was dealing with a person who dabbled in property crime, a different person, not unlike many who live off the beaten path. My view of this man changed rapidly, though, after I realized who he was and how close I also came to becoming a victim of his.

The investigation and prosecution of David Shearing was a team effort involving many highly skilled and dedicated police officers. I was one of many. My job was to deliver Shearing up to the homicide investigators, and they did the hard slogging that transformed a suspect into a convicted killer. One might think that a sense of satisfaction derived from helping solve such grisly crimes would be a talking point for the rest of one's career and well into retirement. Not really.

What has lived with me since the events of 1981 are the senseless nature of the crimes, the horror that the victims suffered, and the tremendous toll that survivors, family, and friends, continue to endure. There is no cure for this pain. Through the years, I have maintained contact with some of those who grieve, and that has been both heartwarming and therapeutic for me. I hope it has been for them as well. This case was a life-changing event for me. Despite the depravity and wanton lack of humanity demonstrated by the killer, I have come to meet many special people who populate the pages of this book.

Murder Times Six is a must-read book on a number of levels. Not only does it shine a spotlight on crimes that captured the attention of a nation, but it is also the narrative of a complex police investigation and a discussion of whether a convicted mass murderer should ever be released back into society. Most importantly, it is the story of one extended family changed forever. But books must be more than a recitation of what occurred. There must be a greater purpose, or why bother. Here there is a more fundamental reason why I commend this book to you. It exposes the worst and the best in our society. We view our country as part of the developed world, yet we still fall victim to the worst depravity. How can this be? Is the answer within ourselves, and in this case, within David Shearing? Or is there more? Why do we not know what motivates people like Shearing to do what they do? When will we understand to a degree of certainty that is more than what we need to convict and send a person to prison? These are the real questions.

I enjoyed every day of my RCMP career, and most of my colleagues would say the same thing. For all the horror and sadness, we always saw the bright spots: the people who persevere and move on but never forget, the diligent investigators who never give up even when it all seems hopeless, and those such as Alan Warren, who chronicle cases like this so that they are not forgotten. In a clear, cogent, and concise manner, Alan has written a book that encourages readers not only to turn pages but to contemplate the meaning behind those pages. He leaves us with that seemingly unanswerable question, can we let this man ever leave the confines of an institution? To that question, we could add another. How do we prevent others from sinking to the depths of this man? Ultimately, how do we and those who come after us learn from this tragedy?

Ron German, Sgt. RCMP (retired)
October 1, 2020

Rick Webber- Global News Anchor, CHBC-TV, Kelowna B.C

It was a crime, or a series of crimes, unlike anything seen in British Columbia. The horror of the Johnson-Bentley murders almost forty years ago cut across generations. For parents, grandparents, and children, it was their worst fears come to life.

As a broadcast journalist working in the southern interior in the early 80s, I clearly remember how the crime and the ensuing investigation gripped the entire region. It seemed like a long, suspenseful wait for all of us, from the time of the families' disappearance to the arrest of a suspect. During that period, as the extent of David Shearing's crimes came to light, new and painful revelations were revealed. As a result, even a generation of campers who had believed their biggest worry in the BC backcountry was garbage-hunting bears, suddenly became concerned for their safety.

Decades later, reminders of the "Wells Gray Murders" continue to persist. Such as when children visit the Johnson Bentley recreation center in West Kelowna, or when David Ennis, formerly Shearing, comes up for parole. The residual and devastating impact of the murders on family members and friends drew author Alan Warren to this story many years later.

As you would expect, *Murder Times Six* provides a clear and detailed account of the crime, the victims, the investigation, even the officers involved in solving the case. But to me, the book's most significant value is that it accomplishes what day-to-day journalism doesn't. It provides context. What kind of life and background could have led a man to commit such acts? Why does the system allow him to apply for release repeatedly? Even the effectiveness of treatment options for pedophiles is examined.

I found parts of this book difficult to read, specifically when describing what happened to the children. But I also learned a lot, especially about how the police investigation unfolded and how Shearing was convinced to confess. *Murder Times Six* provides a valuable new perspective on one of BC's most horrendous crimes and the impact that continues to this day.

Rick Webber
October 5, 2020

PREFACE

On a windy Fall day, I traveled to a salon in Kelowna, B.C, called Sass, where I always drop in for a visit and leave a few of my true crime books for the stylists working there. This time the owner of the salon approached me and asked why I had never written about the murders that happened to a local family back in the eighties.

Quite often, I am asked how I find out about the true crime stories I have written, and this would be a perfect example. Someone asks me a question about a murder, usually just to get my take on what happened and who committed the crime. If it sounds interesting, when I return home, I do an internet search on the crime to find out if others had already written about it, when it was written, and check to see if there's any other recent information.

If I find some interest in the case, I then start looking for as many records I can get my hands on, such as police files, court records, and any media coverage of the crime. Then I'll search for anybody who was connected to the crime, such as family members or police and send them messages to see if they would like to contribute. And then I wait.

In this particular case, it was several months before I received any responses. But when I did, they were all very willing to participate and could even help me find more witnesses who would also love to be a part of the book. It was at this point that I decided to move forward on the case and began my interviews.

On August 2, 1982, three generations of a family set out on a camping trip to Wells Gray Park located in the interior of British Columbia, Canada. The park is located about 300 miles northeast of Vancouver and 465 miles northwest of Calgary and has a total area of 5,250 square kilometers.

The family included Bob and Jackie Johnson, their two daughters, Janet and Karen, and Jackie's parents, George and Edith Bentley. They were all set to meet up at the Old Bear Creek Prison site. When the Johnsons arrived in their car, they set up a tent for their two daughters to sleep in. The Bentleys were bringing their new camper for the adults.

The last time they would be heard from was on August 6, when Edith called another of her daughters. On August 16, Bob was scheduled to return to his job at the Gorman Brother's Lumber, located in West Kelowna, but he didn't show up. This was very unusual behavior for Bob, and his supervisor tried calling his house several times, with no answer. About a week later, Bob's boss ended up calling the police and reported the situation to them.

The mass murder that took place had far-reaching impacts on the family, the community, and even the country. And still does today. This book is not only about the Johnson and Bentley families and what happened to them on that fateful trip. It is also about justice when it comes to murder. The killer, in this case, is eligible for parole. He has been since 2008 but has been denied twice. But should a mass murderer be paroled after killing six people?

It is my hope that this book will bring awareness to the fact that the killer is not only living a somewhat comfortable life with a wife but that he will be eligible for parole again in 2021. The usual reaction I hear from this is, "There's no way a murderer of six people will get out on parole!" or "people like that never get out."

On July 23, 2020, Leslie Van Houten was found suitable for parole (i.e., recommended that she be paroled) at a hearing by the California Board of Parole Hearings. This was her fourth consecutive parole recommendation. For those of you that don't remember who she was or what she was convicted of, let me remind you.

Van Houten was sentenced to death in 1971 for her part in the August 10, 1969 murders of Leno and Rosemary LaBianca. Van Houten was 19 when she and other cult members of Charles Manson fatally stabbed the LaBiancas, carved up their bodies, and smeared the couple's blood on the walls. In 1972, her sentence was commuted to life after the California Supreme Court outlawed the death penalty, stating it was unconstitutional. Since 1978, Van Houten has been eligible for parole and has been denied 19 times.

In Van Houten's parole hearings, she always describes a troubled childhood and how she was devastated when her parents divorced when she was only 14. She claimed to have started hanging out with the wrong crowd and abusing drugs. At 17, she quit school and ran away from home with her boyfriend, and that was when she got involved with Manson.

Shearing has used the same kinds of excuses to justify his criminal past. But now he claims to have found God and is sorry for his crimes, and would like to finish out his life with his wife (who he married since he went to prison) and doing some good in the world.

I am glad that Shearing has found his redemption in God and feels his apology is sufficient atonement to be allowed to finish out the rest of his life back in regular society. But I really think the question we need to answer is 'Do we want people who commit such violent crimes, like murder and rape, out in free society?'

Would you want him living next door to you?

PART I

1

NEVER FORGET HER EYES

"A family is about to go on a journey, to a world that they've never known, to a strange and dark place, only to come across a man that until now, was just a shadow in their eyes."

George and Edith Bentley with Bob Johnson and his daughters Janet and Karen

Bob Johnson, 44, was excited to tell his neighbors and coworkers about the two-week camping trip he was about to take with his wife Jackie, 41, and their two daughters Janet, 13, and Karen, 11. They planned to go to Jasper National Park in Alberta with Jackie's parents, George and Edith Bentley, who lived in Port Coquitlam, B.C. Bentley had just recently retired from his job in a lumber mill and bought a brand-new heavy-duty 1981 silver Ford pick-up truck with a 10-foot Vanguard over the cab camper. He also put an aluminum boat on top of the camper and hung an outboard motor on the back. "This trip would be the first time that they ever went to Wells Gray Park. They heard it was beautiful and wanted to go camping there," explained Kelly Nielsen, the Bentley's granddaughter. George, 66, and Edith, 59, had decided it was the time in their lives to go out and enjoy the beautiful scenery and parks that Canada had to offer them. "My own parents were thinking of going on that same camping trip but opted to go to Port Alberni instead," Nielsen said.

Johnson planned to meet the Bentleys in Clearwater, near the head of the North Thompson River, high in the Columbia Mountain Range of the Rocky Mountains. The Johnsons were bringing a tent and sleeping bags for the girls, and the Bentley camper would be where the adults slept. "I'm going to get in some of the best fishing of my life," Bob Johnson told everyone around him who would listen, "And it will be a great outdoor experience for the girls."

The Johnson family packed most of their camping gear in a car-top carrier on their 1979 Plymouth Caravelle and left on Monday, August 2, 1982. Their first stop was to visit their friends located in Red Deer, Alberta. The Bentleys checked into a campsite about 250 miles northwest of Calgary on August 8, and the Johnsons arrived on August 11. Sometime after that, they all headed to Wells Gray Park together.

They preferred to be away from any crowds or large groups, so instead of going to the main park campsites, they set out to find something 'off the beaten track.' A quiet and secluded place to camp, but still close to the fishing. When they came across the old-abandoned prison site, they knew it was perfect. It was already pretty clear of debris and had reasonably flat ground, perfect to put the tent and camper on. It wouldn't have taken very long to unload the camper on four flat cement pads they found at the site, and the girls were so excited to start their adventure in the outdoors, they set the tent up in minutes.

The first night was clear and warm, with no clouds. As they sat around their campfire, they made plans to go fishing the next morning. The two girls were worried about their dog, Tyke, which had gone missing from their home a few days before they left for their camping trip. They couldn't help but miss having him along with them. They both wanted to sleep with him in their tent and take him out on the water when they went fishing and swimming. Their mother, Jackie, had to come up with different explanations as to what happened to their dog, assuring them that he was safe, and probably back at home waiting for them to return.

The next morning came real early for the girls. They were so excited they could hardly wait for the sun to rise. They dressed in their swimsuits and were ready to go before the adults were up to make breakfast. Their day was spent running through the woods, exploring, and enjoying the nature surrounding them, with not a care in the world. They even each caught a small fish in the afternoon. But on their way back to show their parents, they saw movement among the trees outlining their camp. They figured it must have been an animal like a deer and didn't pay it much attention. They continued on back to their camp.

That night they all enjoyed sitting around the campfire talking about all the things they had seen that day and what they planned to do the next. They planned to check out the old prison site to see if they could see any ghosts.

This was a great summer for the family. Janet had just finished seventh grade, and when they returned from their vacation, she would be going into high school. A few years younger, Karen had just completed Grade 5 and would be going into Grade 6. They were so excited about life.

Grandmother Bentley loved to cook and bake, not just for her and her husband, but also for everyone else. One of her specialties was huckleberry pie, and this was the perfect place to find the berries. The next morning started out bright and sunny, so she took the two girls to where the old prison site was to play and get her berries.

About mid-day, the wind started up. It was not

much more than a light but constant breeze, but there were pretty strong gusts every once in a while. The girls were lost in their imaginations and role-playing all through the prison grounds, while Edith collected the berries she needed for her pie. They soon went back to the camp to make dinner and have another campfire with the whole family.

Once everyone ate and washed up, it was time to talk about what a great day they all had and get excited for what they had in store for tomorrow. After a few stories, the girls were tired and yawning so much, they could hardly talk. Their mother, Jackie, helped them wash up, get into their tent, and ready for bed. After they were all set, she let them come back out to the campfire, get a roasted marshmallow, and say "good night" to everyone.

About a half-hour passed. The girls were whispering to each other about what they saw that day. They were almost asleep when suddenly a loud crash startled them both. "What was that?" Karen questioned. Janet slowly turned to face where the tent door was, and Karen followed her gaze.

Suddenly, there was a lot of screaming and yelling. It was hard to tell what the voices were saying, as the tent walls muffled the voices. The only thing they could tell was that it sounded like both men and women adults who were doing the talking. Then, two more crashing sounds, one right after another. But those sounded a bit further away than the first crashing sound.

Janet started to unzip the tent door slowly and made it half-way before she realized someone else from the outside was trying to unzip the tent door at the same time. She could see the shape of the person from the campfire, and it looked like her mother. Just as they both managed to get the zipper far enough down to see each other's eyes, another crashing sound came. This one was so close that Janet jumped in fear and fell backward. When she got back up, her mother was gone, and the camp went completely silent.

Both girls jumped back, screaming loudly. A minute later, that must have felt like an hour, went by. Another figure approached the outside of the tent door. Slowly, a hand finished unzipping the door to the tent. Two much larger hands opened up the tent door and a man's face came through.

2

FAR AWAY FROM HOME

"The grey light of early morning brings no relief, at least the night has passed, a night that was touched with fear."

Bob and Jackie Johnson with their daughters Janet and Karen

On August 23, 1982, Al Bonar, manager of the Gorman Mills in West Kelowna, B.C., placed a phone call to the RCMP detachment in Kelowna. He was reporting a long-term missing employee by the name of Bob Johnson. "Bob hasn't taken a sick day, let alone missed a day's work by just not showing up in 20 years," he explained to the officer. "They had gone on a camping vacation with his family to Wells Gray Park about two weeks ago and haven't returned. He has missed almost a week of work now. The family was scheduled to return on the 16th of August."

The missing person's report was forwarded to Sergeant Baruta of the Clearwater detachment. Baruta checked around the local park and businesses to see if he could find out anything. The Bentleys had given them photos to pass around as well. The report was also sent out to the Kamloops detachment, where sergeant Mike Eastham headed up the Serious Crime Unit for the interior of B.C. Never in his life did Eastham expect to be in charge of one of the most expensive missing person investigations in Canadian history. He always knew he wanted to be an RCMP officer, and by 14-years old, he had made up his mind. Then, he was transferred to Kamloops at about the twenty-year mark with them.

"There was a lot of speculation as to what really happened to them. Anything from they had run away to join a cult, they were lost, joined a commune, or something like that. Everybody had their fingers crossed, hoping that they were going to be found safe and sound. And as it was, it didn't turn out that way. Six innocent lives gone, like that," Eastham said.

The first tip they received came from a local gas station located about 40 miles east of Clearwater. The attendant, Reg Bedard, remembered seeing the grandparents, George and Jackie traveling with their two grandchildren. They had stopped at the Avola PetroCan to refuel their truck and asked the attendant if she knew of a good place to pick berries while there.

The police led a search that included help from the community, including private pilots and Clearwater residents. The search went on for weeks to no avail.

"I was thinking maybe an accident happened, and they were unable to get help, or they were trapped in an area because it's so dense up there," Kelly Nielsen, the Bentleys' granddaughter explained. "After a few days, I started to worry more. Uncle Bob would have found some way to get some sort of help if they were in any kind of trouble. Watching the news every day gets frustrating and difficult. I remember one time my mother standing in the kitchen, washing dishes, and she just started to cry."

Finally, on September 13, 1982, an Abbotsford man, Kurt Krack, remembered seeing the Johnson vehicle while he was out picking mushrooms in the Wells Gray Park sometime in late August. He claimed he had seen a burnt-out Chrysler in the woods, just off the Battle Mountain Road.

Sergeant Baruta headed up to the location that Krack had described to him. It was basically a horseback riding trail, almost too rough for an average car or truck. From the road, Baruta could see tire marks running off the road into the bush. He stopped his vehicle and got out to follow the tire marks. It wasn't long before he saw the outline of what looked like a burnt-out car.

Once they got to about 150-feet away, he could see the license plate enough to read the numbers.

"Yes, this is the one," he said with an anguished sigh. When the officers approached the vehicle, they glanced inside and what they saw caused them to rope it off and call in the homicide team immediately.

At 10 a.m., Eastham was at a diner talking with other detectives when he received a phone call. Odd because whoever was calling had to know he was there. But remember, this was the time before cell phones or pagers, so this was the way people communicated. Over the phone, a voice yelled, "Mike, the inspector is looking for you now! The inspector said to tell you to get your ass up here quick. We have a major problem!"

3

IT'S ALL DECIDED FOR US

"When hope is gone there is nothing, and the world becomes an empty void, for one family, the setting sun indicates the beginning of a long and lonely night, haunted by the thoughts of the missing."

The Johnson's 1979 Plymouth car was found

They all went back to the detachment, where the inspector told them the news. "We have information that a vehicle bearing the same license plate number as the missing Johnson's car has been found. It has been completely burnt-out, and they believe there are bodies in it."

Wells Gray Park was British Columbia's second-largest park with over one million acres. It was amazing that anybody would find one burnt-out car hidden in the bushes in such a large area, with so few police officers working the crime. Sergeant Baruta did a great job keeping everyone else away from the scene of the crime. The press had somehow already found out about the missing car being found and its location. Several media helicopters were flying overhead trying to get pictures, and even more media crawled all over the area in vehicles, trying to find the correct location.

Eastham approached Baruta and asked him what they were dealing with. Baruta removed his sunglasses and started to explain. "Well Mike, what it appears to be is a burnt-out vehicle. There's absolutely nothing left inside. It's completely burnt out. The shell appears to be intact, and it looks like there's human skeletal remains in the back."

Eastham said, "Walking towards that car, you could feel it, I don't want to say that you could smell a death, but you could smell the death. And you just knew what you were going to walk into." Eastham approached the car with the forensic identification team. "You know you're going to be looking at something that you don't want to see. You know it's going to be smelly; you know it's going to be somebody's life that's been snuffed out."

The team would have to remove the remains without damaging any of them. "When I looked into that car, into the back seat, you could see some bone fragments, and it was evident that it had been a person. At that point in time, we didn't know if it was one or two people in the back of that car." The officers kept their eyes out for any type of evidence that might be located on the ground around the car.

The Johnson vehicle was a 1979 cream-colored Plymouth. What should have been a fairly new car now looked like an old burnt-out rust bucket that had been in a field for twenty years. There was broken glass all around the car, probably pieces from the headlights, taillights, or missing back window. The ground was scorched for about 20-feet all around the car. It had burned so hotly that the door handles and all four tires had melted away. The car doors were all closed except for the driver-side door, which had been left open. On top of the car, there was some sort of carrier the family probably used to carry their camping supplies. What remained was just burnt-out cans and bottles. They figured whoever burned the car like this was probably storing gasoline or some other accelerant.

The trunk was closed, but in the lock was a key ring with five keys attached to it. When Eastham got close enough to the trunk to look at the keys and lock mechanism, he noticed a dusty smell. At first, he figured the smell was coming from the four dead bodies piled into the back seat. But it was now time to see what was in the trunk.

The trunk's mechanism was rendered useless from the fire, so Eastham grabbed a crowbar and pried it open. The skulls of two children were facing upwards — one of them looking directly at the detective. The skulls rested on what looked like a pile of charred bones. There was a prominent hole just over the left eye area of one of the skulls, possibly an exit wound from being shot in the back of the head. "The sight that we had to look at was indescribable. Two little skeletons, what was left of them. These two little skulls looking at us with their hollow eyes. One of them had what looked to be a bullet exit wound above one of the eye sockets. And it was quite evident at that time that it was the two children Karen and Janet," Eastham explained.

Daryl McNaughton, the RCMP's on-site Pathologist, also described the scene, "We were able to pry open the trunk at that time. Of course, we were faced with two additional bodies. It became obvious quite quickly that they were young people. It appeared that the bodies had been casually stuffed into the backseat...Some of the bones were still recognizable but were fractured. Many of them were virtually ash, so whenever you touched them, they tended to crumble. We felt that probably the best thing for us to do was to remove them as carefully as we could. Tagging them, labeling them, photographing the process as it proceeded...These individuals were probably killed prior to them being placed in the vehicle. The skull was opened, and the bullet was found, and submitted to the lab."

The detectives had to positively identify the bodies that were burned in the car. Initially, it was thought there were only two adult bodies in the back seat, Bob and Jackie Johnson. It seemed obvious that the bodies of their two daughters, Janet and Karen Johnson, were in the trunk.

Thoughts about what happened here swarmed Eastham's mind. He heard the grandfather, George Bentley, carried a 410/.22 over/under rifle in the cab of his truck. Was the family shot and killed with his own rifle? Did they pick up a hitchhiker, or were they approached at the park? It wasn't in the police's minds that this crime would have been just one culprit. A few people must have done this much killing and destruction, maybe three. Was everyone killed at the same time? What was the reason for the slaughter?

Many key questions needed to be answered, but first, they had to find out where the grandparents were and what happened to their truck and camper. It should have been the first vehicle found. After all, it was much bigger than the car, and it had an aluminum boat on the top.

Eventually, the forensics team ended up with about fifty plastic bags, which contained the remains of whoever was killed and burned in the car. There were also a lot of their personal effects, such as jewelry, belt buckle, and a women's wristwatch.

It wasn't long before the forensics team came to sergeant Eastham to inform him there were six skulls, not four. So more than likely, they were already looking at all six bodies of the family that were missing. As well, forensics confirmed one of the skulls from the car's back seat also had a bullet hole through it.

Eastham arranged for the Johnson's and Bentley's homes to be searched to find hair or blood samples, or anything that could be used to match what they found in the car. This was before DNA exploded onto the scene and became law enforcement's most effective crime-solving tool. But eventually, the dental records confirmed who the bodies belonged to.

4

I PROMISE TO TRY

"The death passed through the halls of the school and settled like dust in its corners, spurred by hope, but grounded by fear. The search continues as life itself continues, Not only for the Johnsons and Bentleys, but for the people of this small town."

School Photos of Janet & Karen

It was now early September, and the summer was over. Tuesday, September 7, 1982, was the first day that everyone was to return to school. There's something exciting about starting a new school year for everyone, new teachers, new classmates, and sometimes new friends. But that's not how it was for the kids returning to schools in West Kelowna. It almost felt like getting onto a plane, waiting for some of the people you are traveling with to board, and no matter how much time passed, they never boarded. Now it's time for the plane to take off, and they're still not here.

By now, the rumors were rife. They started as 'their car must have broken down' or 'they must be lost deep in the woods and can't find their way out.' Then, they became grimmer like 'they must have been in an accident or even driven off of a cliff, and they are unable to go for any help because they are too hurt.' Similarly, there were rumors about the family joining some sort of cult and moving far away. Regardless, the fear in everyone's hearts was deep, and the one thing that nobody wanted and tried hard to keep out of their minds was soon about to be exposed, and there'd be nothing else left to say.

The first week of classes had an unmistakable nervous feeling that ran through the students and teachers alike. Every time the phone rang, everyone in the office stopped and waited to hear who was calling. The anticipation kept many from eating their lunches or laughing at jokes told in the halls. When the classes started, it was hard for anybody to focus on the subject of the course. Gerry Kroeker, the now-retired seventh-grade teacher, explained, "It was very hard to be focused on our curriculum. Deep in our minds, we were thinking about the Johnsons. So it felt like I was just skimming over what I had to. I would explain something to the class, and somebody would put their hand up and ask me a question, and I couldn't remember what it was that I had just said."

The kids asked their teachers things they didn't want to ask their parents. Some of the questions they wanted answers to, they figured they probably wouldn't get it from their parents. A lot of the kids talked amongst themselves and shared several stories, but still there were no answers. "I had to try and keep their minds on what we were talking about in class, but it seemed that there would end up being something asked about the Johnson family during the day by a couple of students," Kroeker said.

The following Monday the 13th, when the Johnson's vehicle was discovered, and the police knew there were at least four bodies in the car, the adults in both the Johnson and Bentley families were notified. They contacted their kids as soon as possible to try and protect them from the media. They knew as soon as the news hit the airwaves, the reporters would descend on any of the relatives' homes.

In school, it was up to the teachers in each class to explain to the students what happened to the family. And that was not going to be easy. "At first, we didn't know what happened. We just heard that there were four bodies found in the back of the Johnson car," Kroeker remembered. "They assumed that it was the Johnson family and that the Bentleys were still missing. But what had happened to them, and how did they end up in the back of the car and burned? Was it an accident so bad that the car had burned, and nobody was able to escape? I didn't know, and I didn't want to make up a story."

Schools back in the 70s and 80s were not equipped to deal with such things like the brutal murder of neighbors. Why would they be? How many times did something like this ever happen? So, it was left to the teachers to try and answer the questions the children would have. They had to try explaining what was truly unexplainable. Psychologists and psychiatrists were not a standard health service back then, and in fact, most people didn't trust or believe in therapy. Even if a parent supported seeing a therapist, it wasn't accessible in a small town like West Kelowna. And it wasn't covered by any medical insurances at the time.

"All that week, more information kept coming out and was reported on the news." We had to get the kids away from their homes because as soon as the news hit the airwaves, every reporter would be at their doors," remembered Bob Johnson's twin sister, Elaine Woods. "We felt that it was important to protect the children."

The Johnson and Bentley families were forced into hiding as the media camped out on all their front lawns and driveways. It only added to the tension. All the adults were in shock and were on automatic drive, giving no thought to their daily tasks, just doing them. "We all had hope. We had to have hope. That's all we had. George and Edith could still be alive. It was hard to believe, but I promised to try," Woods said.

5

NIGHT COMES DOWN

"We have mourned and wept for those who have passed on. Our tears have dried, but our hearts are scarred indelibly. Life continues although our memory serves to freshen the wound. We are therefore vulnerable to the great shock that a sudden return can bring."

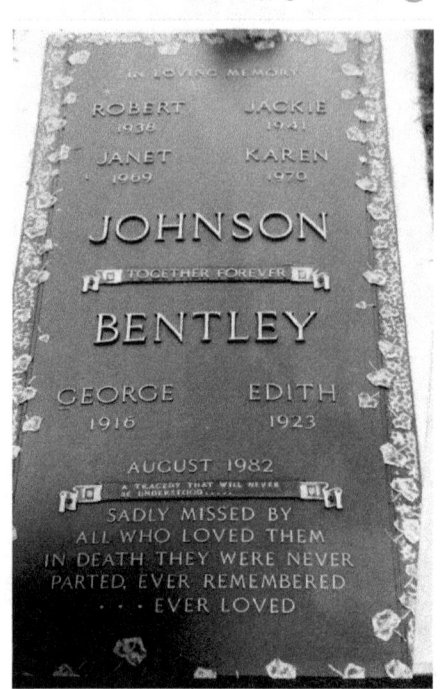

About ten days after the bodies were found, the family decided to hold a funeral service for their loved ones, even though it wasn't until sometime in October before the police forensics unit in Vancouver released the victims' remains. It took them a long time to positively identify the bodies, and it was primarily from Bob Johnson and Edith Bentley's dentures.

On September 23, at St. Paul's United Church on Pandosy Street in Kelowna, they had a service. Reverend A. Baldeo officiated the 300+ attendees who came to pay their respects to the murdered Johnson and Bentley family members. The service included descriptions of the family:

- **Father, Bob:** "Duty, decency, reliability, honor, dignity, respect: these are all qualities that my father not only held in high esteem but practiced every day during his time on this earth. He was a serious and disciplined man, but he could never resist the opportunity to have a laugh with friends and loved ones, given half the chance."
- **Mother, Jackie:** "She was a vibrant soul, one who literally lit up the room whenever she entered. And right up until she became less able to get around, Mum was full of joy and always eager to help out, no matter what the problem was."
- **Daughters, Janet and Karen:** "It is with so much sadness that I am here today to say farewell to two beautiful little girls. Both lovely and vibrant daughters who have been taken away from us much too early. But the memory of them will live on in us forever. We were so proud of them and know that they are now at peace."

After the funeral service was over, the family returned to the Johnson residence, went through all of their remaining possessions, and decided what they would do with them. Bob and Jackie Johnson lived with their two children, Janet and Karen, on the main floor of their Watt Road home, in West Kelowna. Bob's parents lived in the basement of the house after making it into an in-law suite with its own entrance.

The entire family was in an emotional blackout, and several questions ran through their minds. "There is a part of all of us, I think, that would want to leave the house the way it was, a perfect time capsule. How could we change this house where my family lived? How could we give a single thing away? The answer to every question was that we couldn't, but we had to."

After a death, you can't imagine the world will go on without the person who died, but somehow it does. You imagine you won't be able to put one foot in front of the other, yet somehow you do. You want to hold on to everything forever, but you can't. Eventually, each family member took what they wanted to cherish memories of their lost ones, the larger pieces of furniture were sold, and the remaining items went in a garage sale.

On November 12, the family held a private burial service at the Lakeview Memorial Gardens in Kelowna, also conducted by the Reverend Baldeo.

In late November, Sharlene Johnson, along with

her husband and newborn, decided to move into the house's upstairs. They would be a great help and support to Bob's parents, who had been alone in their basement suite since August when the Johnsons first left for their camping trip.

In this photo from left to right:
Bob Johnson – age 44
Jackie Johnson – age 41
Janet Johnson – age 13
Karen Johnson – age 11

Grandparents George and Edit Bentley

6

THE WAITING SEEMS LIKE ETERNITY

"There was a moment of hope on this night, only to have that hope withdrawn, and despair and further confusion follow."

For the police, the next priority was the search for the truck and camper. The grandparents had a 1981 red and grey Ford pick-up truck carrying a 10½ foot Vanguard camper. It had a picture of an orange sunset painted on the front window. They were also carrying an aluminum boat with a small Evinrude motor on top of the camper.

At first, the police decided to put out an APB on the truck and camper with the license plate number, on the off chance the killers were driving it around the local area, in B.C., or even the U.S. Soon enough, the media got word of the search for the truck and camper and released it to the public. After that, the police were inundated with calls and tips about sightings of the missing truck. Most were throughout Canada, all the way to Quebec even.

The police would also have to try and pinpoint the exact location where the family was camping. After talking with family members, they learned that it would have probably been in a remote part of the park, as they didn't care for the more popular and crowded campsites. One issue facing police was that the family never used credit cards. They didn't believe in them, so finding a paper trail was unlikely.

The police also had their hands full with all of the media attention surrounding this case. Technology at the time was advanced enough that people could watch the details of the investigation unfold right in front of them on their televisions. While beneficial in some ways, it led to the police getting overwhelmed with thousands of tips from viewers. And every one of them had to be checked, using up valuable police time.

The RCMP's Clearwater detachment set up a large-scale search for any information on the family with help from federal and provincial services, civilian volunteers, and even private pilots. They knocked on every door in the area with pictures of the Johnsons, Bentleys, the Plymouth car they were driving, and the truck and camper.

The search led to the first tip on the missing truck and camper. A B.C. resident on vacation in

Saskatchewan recognized the pictures and called the hotline. The witness had actually followed the truck and camper, that still had the boat on top of it, into a gas station and saw two men get out of the truck, not a family. The witness also said that the two men ended up in the same restaurant he was in, and he believed he heard them speaking French.

The two men were described as being in their late twenties, quite shabbily dressed, rugged, with long unkempt hair. The smaller of the two men was blond, and the larger had dark hair. Police decided that they would interview the waitresses and other workers from the gas station and restaurant in Saskatchewan. After that, they had sketches made up for the two suspects.

Another tip came in from one of the Wells Gray Park attendants, who remembered seeing the truck and camper parked at the area known as the "Old Bear Creek Prison site." The prison site was an old mobile prison that had long since been removed. It had taken up about a 3-acre area of the park.

Eastham and his partner took a look around the old prison site and found a few things such as three canning lids that matched the canned goods found on top of the Johnson's burned Plymouth. There were also Extra Old Stock beer bottle caps, which was the kind of beer that Bob Johnson drank all the time.

They decided it would be best to bring in a search team to have a closer look.

The searchers later discovered Extra Old Stock beer placed in a nearby riverbed, probably to keep them cool. They also found six spent .22 shell cartridges. The campfire pit had seats set up for six people, and there were sharpened sticks, probably used for roasting marshmallows at the fire. There were four level blocks laid out at the same site that could have been used to place the camper. It seemed most likely that this was not only the place the family had been camping but also the place where they were murdered.

The rest of 1982 passed without any further movement on the case. By January of 1983, several cash rewards were being offered. $7,500 was offered for information leading to the missing truck, and $35,000 was being offered for information leading to the arrest and conviction of the person(s) responsible for the deaths of the Johnson and Bentley families.

By the end of April of 1983, the case started to become cold. There was almost no new tips or calls coming in about the murders or the missing truck. So, the police came up with a new approach – a publicity campaign lasting one month. It involved driving across Canada with a truck and camper that were the same as the one owned by the Bentleys. This drive happened at the same time as a reenactment of the crime was televised. Eastham explained, "when you come to a dead-end, you gotta come up with some pretty creative ideas on how the hell you are going to move forward. How are you going to keep this in the public's mind? People care about what happens in their own homes, in their backyard. But if you live in Manitoba, you don't pay attention to the B.C. news."

RCMP Constable Gerald Dalen and Constable DeWitt were the officers chosen to drive the truck across Canada. "We had to make it personal, and we needed to make it local all across the country." The trip started on May 9, 1983. They were going to drive from Kamloops to Montreal in about three weeks. At each stop, they handed out sketches of the two French-speaking male suspects that had been identified the year before.

The road trip started to become extremely popular throughout the country. There were crowds of people waiting for their arrival in many of the cities where they stopped. It became the most crucial part of the trip, as it put the unsolved murders in the spotlight and kept people talking about them. After the 15-day trip ended, the police were again receiving the same number of tips and calls that they had received when the murders first happened.

During the trip, RCMP received over 1,300 tips from people that seemed to have had their memories jogged from seeing the truck and camper replica drive through their towns. One, in particular, caught the ear of Eastham. It came from a mechanic out of Windsor, Ontario. He claimed that two men drove up to his shop in the middle of the night. They had just unloaded their camper and were looking for a quick paint job for their truck and offered him cash to do it.

The men waited at the shop the whole time the mechanic painted their truck for them. During their conversations with the mechanic, they showed him a .22 caliber rifle and a Saturday Night Special handgun. They told him they needed to get rid of them. The mechanic told them that he wanted nothing to do with it as he had had some trouble with the law before and wanted to stay straight. The two men became very stand-offish with him and asked him if he knew where they could go and get rid of the rifle. The mechanic sent them to someone located across the U.S. border in South Detroit, Michigan.

Eastham said, "This guy described the truck as having modifications to the front and rear bumpers. George Bentley had made similar modifications to his truck before his trip to Wells Gray Park. Nobody knew this, and so this mechanic's information looked good, and he had to be telling the truth."

Eastham, wanting to get a quick answer, called

the Detroit Homicide unit directly, avoiding the red tape that would arise if he went through the proper channels that included Interpol and the FBI. Detroit Homicide verified the information he had received from the mechanic, so Eastham decided it was time to go to Detroit.

While he was making his trip plans to Detroit, Eastham received a phone call from Sgt. Baruta of the Clearwater detachment. "Mike, we found it! The truck and camper."

Eastham was in shock, "Where?"

"A couple of forest rangers. They were aware of it because of the press coverage," replied Baruta.

"There's no way! We've been following them across the country, and just got a tip that they were in Detroit," said Eastham.

"Yeah, well, I'm looking at it right now. It's here. The license plate is the only thing not burned, and it reads 4836FY. You need to come home!" Eastham and Leibel immediately flew back to Kamloops to speak with the forestry workers who discovered the truck and look over the area where it was found.

7

NO PLACE LEFT TO HIDE

"The dawn will appear soon and bring with it the unresolved troubles of another day. A frightening and violent man, and the fears that he created have not yet been found, and wherever he is, some violence is surely taking place."

| Burned out Truck and Camper found

Detective Ken Leibel, also known as "Reliable Leibel," was on Eastham's Special Crimes Unit and worked closely with Eastham. He explained, "We had, I believe, in excess of 1,200 tips of people reporting the sightings of this truck, so we kept following those leads as it was all that we had to work with." He shrugged his shoulders in a way a child does when they've done something wrong. "We believed that we knew something about this, and the police can only be as good as the information we received. How do you explain it? People wanting to help would see a truck that looked like the Bentley's, or they saw part of a license plate number that matched? But the bottom line was that we've just wasted a whole year, and my god, it's embarrassing. It was right in our own backyard. But that's the way it goes. It's a new day."

On Tuesday, October 18, 1983, the next big break happened. Two forestry workers, Douglas Kehler, 33, and Peter Miller, 31, walked into the RCMP's Clearwater detachment and said they had found the burnt-out Bentley truck and camper up Trophy Mountain. It was at about the 4,700-foot level.

Eastham walked into the interview room with one of the forestry workers and asked, "So, when exactly did you see the truck and camper?"

The worker replied, "A few weeks ago."

"A few weeks ago, why did you wait so long for? It's been all over the news."

"I was staying in a ranger cabin deep in the park. I hadn't been near a TV in a while. I came in as soon as I heard."

When the police first flew over the location, there was only the truck, and it appeared that no camper or boat was there. Eastham could see why the truck was never spotted. Somehow the fire had changed the truck from the original red and grey to an earth-like color. Once the police unit landed the helicopter and was at the site, they could see what was left of the camper as well. A few feet down from the truck was a large canyon, so it was more than likely that the killers wanted to drive it off the cliff. The only thing was they high centered it and got stuck, so they did not make it to the cliff.

Eastham also had Harvard Boswell, an RCMP forensics photographer, on hand. "My responsibility at the scene was mainly to make a photograph record of all the evidence as it was collected. I record the scene at the beginning when nobody else has been in there to examine it yet. When we first got to the scene, we observed a vehicle in a burnt-out condition, extremely burnt-out. It was almost totally destroyed except just the shell." Boswell also captured images of a freshly chopped tree. "You're looking at where a tree had been cut as if the path was trying to be made to where the car ended up, and there was an axe head found in the car."

Bear Creek campsite was an open area, cut out within the bush, and people used it as a wilderness camping spot. "We're looking for evidence we're trying to put somebody at the scene."

Along with them was pathologist Darryl McNaughton, "I recall that there were a large number of police officers, and in approaching these scenes, one has to be very careful that you don't contaminate the scene or destroy it."

There was also a freelance photographer, Douglas McCormick, who had been assigned by the media to cover the story. "This is one of the first murder cases that I was involved in. A major murder case. You leave this little town, Clearwater, and you go out, and you know you're in the woods. There's nothing out there. It was haunting."

Where the truck was located was a clue in itself. It was a good indication that whoever the killers were, they knew the area well enough to plan this. It could mean that the killer was from the Clearwater area or had some family that lived there. Leibel explained, "The biggest thing that stands out in my memory is just the unreal nature of what we were dealing with. It was just so unreal it's hard to describe. Whoever drove it in here was trying to bring it into the bush as far away from that trail. And, as you know, hide it to the best of their ability." Leibel let out a heavy sigh and continued, "We knew that we're going to have one hell of an investigation on our hands to solve."

"We went in there and photographed the truck," Boswell explained. "The pictures show that part of the truck, just the sides, just caved out through, it was that hot. Usually, vehicles don't burn to that extent unless there's something to accelerate the fire. On the passenger's side, there was a .22 caliber bullet hole in the panel door that we photographed. The bullet hole was in the side of the vehicle. We found the cartridge cases; they were photographed where they were found in the grass."

The Vancouver RCMP then removed the remains of the truck and camper from the area and brought them to a Vancouver crime lab to be thoroughly examined.

The most significant findings on or around the burnt-out truck were that somebody had recently planted tree seeds in the ground near the truck. This was interesting because there was a $7,500 reward out for the truck. That would be motivation enough for anyone who merely stumbled across the vehicle to turn it in; motivation enough for anyone except the murderer, that is. It had been all over the news for two weeks when the police made the run with look-a-like truck and camper all across the country.

Eastham and Baruta also found a bullet hole in the passenger side door of the truck. "I'd say we keep this to ourselves," Eastham told Baruta, "That way we weed out any false confessions, or bad tips." The bullet hole was only known to the police and whoever killed the families. The police kept it from the press and the public.

News media coverage of the Bentley truck discovery was harsh. After both the car and truck were located, criticism came from not only people in the community of Clearwater but also from a recently retired RCMP Homicide Detective, Norman Lee, 66, at the time. Lee had conducted several weeks of his own investigation on the crime in the Clearwater region. "The local police operation," he claimed, "ignored the fundamentals of a homicide investigation. The original search was a haphazard affair, done in piecemeal, instead of concentrating in the area of the park." Lee figured that the police had let themselves become distracted by reports of the suspicious French-Canadians that were in the region regularly, for casual work on farms and agriculture. Transient Quebec residents often traveled from town to town, doing fruit picking jobs. They lived in tents, drank, and partied, and locals didn't like that at all.

Lee was also surprised that the detectives would believe that a murderer would take the trouble to hide the bodies and drive across Canada in such a distinctive stolen vehicle. He stated that the police didn't make themselves accessible to the local tips and offers to help. This was apparent as they didn't accept or want any of Lee's help with the case.

About the bullet hole, forensics thought that it was too large to have been a .22. So that left the question of whether or not a .22 was used to kill the families.

In the earlier forensic tests of the burned bodies, there was only one fragment of a bullet left in one of the adult female skulls, not enough to make any positive identification on it. But by the size of the holes in both skulls, the detectives concluded that it was a .22.

The find pumped some new energy back into the investigation, and 20 more officers were assigned to do another door to door canvassing of the Clearwater and Wells Gray areas. Only this time, they were going to contact every single house. Constable Dalen stated, "The area was in a state of shock and disbelief. Something like this just doesn't happen in an area like this."

During this interview phase of the investigation, the name of David Shearing was first brought to the police's attention. An informant decided to call once they heard a story about Shearing running over a man on the Wells Gray Highway a few years previous to this case.

The next day Shearing's name came up again. This time during one of the door-to-door police canvassings of the houses in Clearwater. The detective knocked on the door of an older, one-story ranch-style home, and a gruff looking man came to the door.

"Yeah!" the man said aggressively.

"I'm Officer Haslett."

Then a woman's voice from behind the door

could be heard, "Who is it?"

"Nobody!" the man shouted out his answer while looking behind his front door.

He now looked back at the cop and asked, "What do you want?"

"You may have heard that we recently found the truck that belonged to the Bentleys?"

"Yeah, I heard about that."

Just then, the woman's face peeked out from behind her husband's body, "Is that the one up by Trophy Mountain?" she asked.

The man quickly turned his head towards his wife and scolded her, "He's talking to me!" Then whips his head back towards Officer Haslett. "What about it?"

"Well, we're wondering if maybe you remember seeing anything suspicious. Anything that might help us find out who put the truck there?"

"I already told you guys. I haven't seen anything like that."

"What about you, ma'am?"

The man answers for her. "No, there's nothing."

The woman then looks towards the man and says. "You're not going to tell him about David and the truck that got shot up?"

"This isn't our business!" the man answered angrily.

"I told you everything we're going to tell you."

The officer changed his line of questioning some to try and calm the situation and perhaps learn something else. "Alright, sir, I will leave you my card, and if you can think of anything else, please contact us. Thanks."

The officer told Eastham and Leibel as soon as he got back to the station. "We had investigative two-men teams that would follow up on these types of specific tips. We couldn't really use the polygraph test much as there was the privacy act thing in our way," Leibel explained. "And it couldn't be used in court anyway."

They set up surveillance at the house so they would know when the husband left. And as soon as he did, they picked up the wife and brought her in for questioning. She confirmed the story. "She told us Shearing wanted to know how he could register a vehicle that was stolen, and how he could fix a bullet hole in the door," Leibel confirmed. Eastham added, "She told us that there's a guy by the name of David Shearing and that he lives on a ranch out in the Wells Gray Park Road, and he made mention of finding a vehicle up in the mountain with a bullet hole in the door. All of a sudden, we've got a name, David Shearing, and needed to know who the hell is David Shearing?"

DAVID SHEARING

Shearing had lived on his father's 160-acre hobby farm, located just two miles away from where the bodies of the Johnsons and Bentleys were discovered. He had lived there his whole life until about four months prior to his arrest on November 19, 1983 when he moved to the Tumbler Ridge area to find some work as a laborer.

Shearing's father, William, had worked at the Bear Creek Prison, which was a minimum-security prison, and raised cattle on his farm for extra income for most of his life. David, the youngest of three children, was considered a quiet boy and a good student by his teachers and school friends.

Marvin Tremblay, who was the same age as David, went through elementary and secondary school same time as him. Tremblay claims that Shearing was prolific in both mathematics and mechanics, and when he set his mind to it, he could do just about do anything he tried. "But he was very shy," Tremblay remembers. "You'd have to get very close to him before he would talk to you. He didn't get involved in any of the school activities much. Once in a while, he would show up to a school dance or go to a drive-in movie with him. I heard that he liked to drink beer a lot, but I had never seen him get into any trouble when he drank with me."

Shearing graduated from Clearwater High school in 1977 and enrolled in a heavy-duty mechanics course held at Caribou College in Kamloops. He planned to get a job working in Kamloops, a major stop for big rig trucks traveling from Calgary to Vancouver. But after he completed his course in heavy mechanics, he was unable to find any work. His mother, Rose, 66 at the time, said that her son ended up doing odd labor jobs around the town and area. He even made the ski trails for the Wells Gray Park one year.

Jack Vogels was the Bar Manager of the Wells Gray Hotel in Clearwater, and remembered Shearing coming in the bar, "He was a real loner. He came in now and again for a few beers, but he never had any girlfriends. He didn't even hang around with any of the guys that were in the bar regularly."

Shearing was still living on his father's farm in the Spring of 1982 when his father died of a heart attack. His sister married and remained in the area, but his brother became Deputy Sheriff with the Provincial Government, doing prisoner escorts and court security duties in Prince George. In the early Fall of 1983, Shearing decided to move up to the Tumbler Ridge area.

In 1983, Tumbler Ridge was still a town under construction, so he figured there would be plenty of jobs to do there. If you hadn't been there during this time, it would be hard to imagine the sheer amount of work that was going on there. Quintette was a major coal company set to open in November of 1983. There were over 1,800 people there just to work on their building alone. Other workers were frantically trying to finish houses to live in before the winter hit.

Tumbler Ridge was just one of many towns rapidly being built, usually around some sort of industry mill like coal or oil in the northern parts of B.C. and Alberta. The towns attracted people who were unable to find work for different reasons. Ex-cons accounted for a large percentage of these workers. Because of their status in society, it was a good place to earn money and stay off law enforcement's radar.

Many construction workers were living outside of the town in a series of work camps, which were just small old trailers placed in roughly cleared lots. There were also some construction workers and laborers that didn't want to pay dues to these camps. So they went out into the bush, cleared some land, and made a make-shift cabin in which to live. One of these workers was Shearing, who built a small cabin on someone else's land that was made almost entirely of stolen building supplies from around Tumbler Ridge. He lived there with some recently-acquired friends that he met there.

But Shearing soon found himself unable to keep a

regular job in Tumbler Ridge. Whether it was his attitude, quality of workmanship, or inability to get along with the others, it's hard to say. He soon fell into a group with similar work behaviors as his own. But with a group of men that aren't working, it's hard to eat or drink much. So, they began to steal tools and work equipment from the construction sites at night to survive.

8

EYES OF A STRANGER

"From the moment I arrived in town, I've been surrounded by tension, and now the band has grown tighter, until the small town comes alive, with ghosts of the past that I never knew, ghosts that draw tight fingers around the present."

Shearing's Make-shift Cabin

Road to Shearing's Cabin in Tumbler Ridge

Ron German started with the RCMP in 1975 in Montreal. His career moved him through Powell River, Gold River, Fort St. John before he finally landed in Tumbler Ridge, British Columbia. German towered at 6 foot 2 inches, and weighed about 200 pounds, had piercing eyes that would grip you with his stare.

In the early part of September of 1982, a large yellow Ford pick-up truck passed him on the road. The truck had a missing headlight, which wasn't worth much more than a second glance in Tumbler Ridge. Most of the trucks driven by construction workers were missing headlights, taillights, or had a cracked windshield. So, after a long day, and at 1:25 a.m., the last thing he was interested in was doing a routine vehicle check. But as the truck passed by, Ron's eye caught the two passengers quickly moving their heads up and down and then spotted lots of tools loaded into the bed of the truck. As the truck turned onto Quadra Camp Road heading towards a trailer park, his suspicions got the better of him, and he turned his vehicle around and decided to follow.

As soon as German got behind the truck, he turned on his blue and red dome lights to signal the driver to pull over. The Ford gently pulled to the side of the dirt road and stopped. As German pulled in behind the truck, he spotted the driver exiting and heading towards him, so he quickly opened his door and stood up and told the driver to stay where he was. It was never a good sign when a driver leaped out of his truck and headed for an officer still parking their vehicle. It could have been that the driver was inexperienced and had never been pulled over before. But it also could have been something sinister. German quickly powered on his off-road lights, which helped stop the driver's approach, and blind the passengers seated in the truck.

"Hey there, how are you doing tonight?" German asked politely.

The driver answered with a nervous and shaky, "Not too bad, officer."

"Could I see your driver's license?" German asked.

The driver shrieked, "Sure," and quickly pulled his license out and gave it to German.

German read over the license and handed it back to the driver, "David William Shearing, so where are you headed tonight?"

"Just back to Quadra Camp from work." Shearing continued, "Going to go there for a bit, then head back home." Shearing was very fidgety and looking around everywhere to avoid making eye contact with German.

"Okay," German answered while he started looking the truck over more closely. "So, what's in the back of the truck?"

Shearing slowly answered, "Well, we got some impact tools here, a compressor, some wrenches, and stuff." German looked over the tools as Shearling was listing off the items, and it all matched up pretty well. In all, he figured there was somewhere around $40,000 worth of tools there.

During this exchange, German also noticed the two passengers did not move once, not even to turn around to see what was going on. It gave German a strange feeling. Almost always, passengers tried to see what was going on between a driver and a cop on a road stop like this.

To top things off, what were construction workers working on this late at night? The workers often came in from Dawson Creek, a good hour and a half away, and would have left for home already.

German decided to ask Shearing to get into his police vehicle's back seat, which Shearing did without hesitation. German didn't cuff Shearing but thoroughly searched him with Shearing's consent. He just locked the doors so Shearing couldn't be any threat to him while he checked out the passengers still in the truck, who still hadn't made any moves. He also noticed the passenger seated on the far right had his right shoulder lowered, a good indication he was hiding something.

German walked around the backside of his car and moved towards the truck on its right along a ditch. He knew his vehicle's bright lights would prevent the occupants in the truck from seeing him. He slowly inched his way, taking slow, deliberate steps, hoping he would see what the two men were hiding.

Suspecting they had some sort of firearm on them and wanting to retain the element of surprise, German slowly drew his firearm as he approached the truck window. By now, both passengers were focused on trying to see what was going on behind them. They squinted into the rear-view mirrors but were only blinding themselves from staring into the bright fire lights blaring from German's car. Before they knew it, German was practically on top of them.

He immediately noticed a 30/30 rifle, cocked and lying across their laps facing towards the driver's door. The passenger on the far right had both his knees bent forward, ready to fire if he approached from that side of the car. Very carefully, German slowly moved his firearm, placing it right behind the passenger's ear through the open window. "Don't even think about moving," He said with a sharp tone. "Get your hands on the dash!" Both passengers placed their hands on the dash without hesitation.

German slowly reached around with his free hand to open the truck door, while not moving his eyes from both passengers. He quickly grabbed the 30/30 from the truck and uncocked the hammer to make the rifle safe. Walking back to his vehicle, he found a round in the spout upon inspection of the firearm. He placed the rifle in his car.

German walked back towards the rear of the truck, and with his weapon still drawn, commanded the middle passenger to slowly get out of the truck with his hands above his head. The dirty, messed up man responded quickly as asked and backed toward him. German cuffed him placed him the backseat of his squad car beside Shearing.

Now he had to take the third passenger, the one who probably would have fired at German if he had approached the truck from the driver's side. This guy had the most attitude in the group and showed enough confidence that German figured he might not come easily.

The officer approached the truck from the driver's side before ordering the man out of the vehicle. The man turned his head away from German, so he holstered his weapon. The last thing a cop wants to do is start grappling with a suspect while his gun was in his hand. At first, there was what seemed like a quiet stand-off between the two. Every second felt like an hour. He slowly approached the truck, and with a lightning-quick jump, German leaped towards the truck, grabbed hold of the suspect, forced him out the door, bent him over, and cuffed him. The rapid succession of movements took the suspect by surprise so much that he did not even have a chance to struggle.

German took the two passengers' information and ran a check on them. The first passenger he cuffed gave a fake name, but eventually, he figured out he was Wyman Laitenan. Once German retrieved some of the serial numbers from the tools in the truck's back, he decided to let Shearing and Wyman go. There was no tool theft reported and no warrants outstanding on those two men. But he arrested the third passenger for the attempted murder of a peace officer. Before leaving for Dawson Creek, German found out that Shearing lived about five miles out of town in a homemade shack.

The following morning, German received a phone call from one of the engineer trailers in camp, reporting a break-in the previous night, where a lot of their tools had been stolen. The Dawson Creek detachment only had three RCMP members working in it, and German had been alone for the last few days. This lack of police resources kept him close to town and following his standard routine, instead of keeping his eyes for that yellow Ford pick-up truck he had pulled over the night before. Mike Johnson, one of the other officers that worked there, returned the next day. After German explained what had happened when he was off, the two decided to go find Shearing, and hopefully, the stolen tools.

The two officers split up in two vehicles to cover more area, and drove through the bush on the rough gravel roads that lined the work camps for a few hours before they spotted a homemade shack. They stopped, parked just out of sight, and got out of their suburban truck to get a closer look. They came upon two men digging a hole in the ground. Beside them was the yellow Ford pick-up truck.

The officers went back to their truck and headed toward the shack at full speed, with sirens and lights blaring. The men dropped their shovels and made a run for it. Johnson quickly came to a stop, skidding his suburban sideways. They jumped out of the cab and started pursuing the men.

The two men led the officers on a lengthy and frantic chase that didn't end until both officers fired a warning round from their weapons through the woods. Seconds later, German tackled Shearing and Johnson caught the second suspect, who turned out to be Fred White, the same guy German booked for attempted murder just two nights before. How did he get out and back here so quickly, German wondered?

After the two were cuffed, the officers started to drag them back to the suburban asking them questions on the way. "Where's your friend, Dave?" German shouted out.

"Fuck you!" Shearing returned at him.

"Is he in the house?"

"No!"

"Let's go check," German responded sarcastically.

"You can't force me to go in there!" Shearing yelled back at him.

That was just what German needed to hear. He grabbed Shearing by the cuffs and forced him in through the shack's front door. Only, Shearing started calling out, "Willie! It's me, Willie!"

German then saw Wyman Laitenan sitting in the corner under a wooden bunk, pointing a .303 at them. Once Wyman noticed German, he threw his weapon out onto the floor in front of them, shouting, "I'm unarmed!"

Johnson returned from putting White into the suburban and grabbed Shearing so German could get Wyman cuffed as well. They took the two back to the suburban and placed them in it. Then they took the three men on the 2-hour trip back to Dawson Creek and booked them for possession of stolen property.

German discovered that White was released because the corporal on duty disagreed German had the right to book him on attempted murder just because he had a rifle lying across his lap, cocked and pointed at the driver's side car door, while German was conducting a stop.

9

I'M A DANGER TO MYSELF

"The residents of town are aware of a strange man in their midst. A man who's presence is felt by all. Others that are far away are soon to be aware of his presence, are soon to be aware of the danger that surrounds him."

Shearing in front of his trailer in Quadra Camp

One day, while German was chatting with Jesse Harrison, the manager of the Quadra Camp trailer park, he heard some interesting things about David Shearing. So he decided to make a note. Shearing had been behind in rent, and the last few times Jesse had gone to him to collect the money, Shearing told him that he was not only going to burn down the camp, but he was going to kill the owner of the trailer park, Joseph LeBlanc. The threat actually scared LeBlanc into taking a stress leave from the camp. Shearing had also bragged about derailing a train, but German had never heard of it. Even stranger were the many stories going around from some of the women in the camp about Shearing and his unnatural sexual behaviors.

After Dawson Creek, Shearing was set free since he did not have a criminal record. He did have to make an appearance once a week to the RCMP detachment, though. He maintained a good record by always showing up on time. During one of Shearing's regular weekly visits to the detachment, news broke about the police finding the Johnson family's missing truck. As Shearing was signing his papers, German piped up, "Look at that. They finally found the truck and camper!"

After Shearing finished his paperwork, he responded, "Really! Where?"

"Oh, right in the park. Imagine that, after all that looking, it just sort of popped up on a mountainside. Pretty amazing!"

"Yup, bushes are pretty thick over there, hard to see down on the ground. I used to live near there."

"Really?" German answered, sounding like he was looking for an answer.

"Yeah, those murders happened a couple of miles away from my house. Really a shock to everyone there." Shearing answered as he left the office.

In the meantime, on November 21st, Shearing was scheduled to appear in court for the possession of stolen property charges. His two friends, who were arrested at the same time as he was, were both in prison for other charges unrelated to this case.

On November 17th, German received more information on a stolen 3000-watt home light generator. He and his corporal headed out to make a visit to Shearing. Not only to see if they could find the generator but to make sure that he was still around and planning on coming in for his court date.

When they arrived around 9:30 that morning, the officers pounded on the door. One of Shearing's friends, Jason Hill, answered.

"Sorry to get you guys up so early," German said to him with a smile in his voice.

"No problem," came from the voice of Shearing from within the house. He had been sitting on his bed, smoking a cigarette before getting up and coming to the door.

"You've got court coming up on Monday!" German continued with enthusiasm.

"Yeah," Shearing mumbled back at him.

"What are you going to do?"

"Well, I am going to plead guilty to the possession charge."

"You have a lawyer?"

"Sort of, I've got legal aid."

As German and his corporal left, they checked in the back of Shearing's truck, where they spotted the stolen generator. The two of them decided not to say or do anything about it. Sgt. Eastham had stayed in contact with them and let them know that Shearing was now a suspect in the Johnson Bentley murders. It was probably better to leave it there for now and use it later as a reason to bring Shearing into town if they needed to question him about the murders.

German called into the Kamloops detachment and told Eastham about the newest details they had on Shearing. Eastham and some other detectives were coming into Dawson Creek the next day and asked them to get Shearing into custody to question him.

The next day, when German spotted Shearing's truck, he pulled him over. Driving was Jason Hill, and along with Shearing, there was a girl. He arrested Shearing for the possession of the stolen generator and booked him in jail. Eastham did not want Shearing held for the murders of the Johnson Bentley families and wanted to have the element of surprise on him when they interviewed Shearing.

Unfortunately, the prosecutor in Dawson Creek didn't go along with Eastham's wishes. After charging Shearing with another charge of possession of stolen property, he released him with a promise to appear.

Knowing that Sergeant Eastham was coming up to question Shearing about the Johnson Bentley murders, the Dawson Creek detachment kept Shearing under surveillance. But just as Eastham was about to arrive, Shearing and Hill jumped on a bus to head back to Tumbler Ridge. Eastham called German and asked him to go to Tumbler Ridge and bring Shearing back to town, but he was not to arrest him or tip him off that he was now a suspect in the Johnson Bentley murders. This left German with the problem of how to talk Shearing into coming with him to Dawson Creek.

After several delays due to bad winter weather, Sgt. Eastham and three other detectives finally arrived in Dawson Creek on November 19th. They checked into a hotel and got some rest. The next morning they were all set to start their interrogation of Shearing.

Shearing had been bussing himself to Dawson Creek with his friend, Jason Hill; the two arriving in the afternoon. German was alone in town again, so he called up their volunteer Auxiliary Constable, Al Kjemhus. After briefing him on the high-risk arrest, German had him stand behind the passenger door of the squad car with a shotgun in hand but out of sight, ready to either use it or operate the action as Shearing would know the sound of a shotgun racking a shell. It would be a deterrent to any violence during the encounter with Shearing or Hill. They were the last two off of the bus and were unhappily surprised to see the police there.

"How are you guys doing?" German said in a very professional manner. The two men didn't answer but nodded as if to say okay.

"Would you mind stepping over to the police car for a minute?" The two slowly wandered over towards the police car before saying anything.

"You're not going to arrest us, are you?" Hill begrudgingly asked.

German looked directly at Hill and said, "Actually, I'm going to arrest you! There's an outstanding warrant out for you under the name of Hardwood."

Quickly, Hill blurted out, "That's not my name! It's Hill!"

"No, it isn't." German replied, "You're under arrest."

German then searched Hill before he cuffed him and placed him in the back of the squad car.

During this whole time, German was focused on how he would get Shearing back to the detachment for questioning without letting him know anything about Eastham and his team of detectives.

"You don't want to talk to me?" Shearing asked of German after Hill's arrest was complete.

"Yes, actually." German quickly answered before Shearing could walk away.

"You wouldn't know anything about some road

damage that was caused by some idiot who walked a D-8 Cat from the BC Rail Service yard to the foot of the trail that leads to your cabin? The cleats of the Cat had torn up the road, and the Department of Highways was really pissed about it!"

"Nah, I don't know anything about it," Shearing replied.

"All right, but members of the Dawson Creek detachment want to talk with you."

Shearing got really annoyed and said, "About what?"

"Other matters," German replied.

Shearing replied, getting even angrier, "You aren't going to arrest me, are you?"

Wanting to calm things down some and keep Shearing from knowing what was really going on, he calmly answered, "No, I won't need to arrest you if you come on your own."

"You wouldn't lie to me, would you?"

"No," German said even though he knew that he would arrest him if Shearing resisted.

"You did before!"

"When?" German asked in a confused state.

"Well, it wasn't you."

"Look, I'll drive you down there, and when they're done talking with you, I'll drive you back up here."

That seemed to relax Shearing some, "Well, okay then."

German grabbed his briefcase and his dog, an Old English Sheepdog named Max. The dog got in the back seat and Dave got in the passenger seat of the car and asked if he had to wear a seatbelt.

"Yes, you have to wear a seat belt." They had some small talk for the first 45 minutes until they came across a dead moose on the road's side. To keep Shearing thinking that things were pretty casual, German stopped to take a look. The two of them stepped out of the truck and went over to the carcass.

"Jason [Hill] said that he saw this on his way in," Shearing brought up.

The two talked about roadkill for a few minutes, then got back to the truck and continued their trip to Dawson Creek. A little bit further down the road, they came across a pack of coyotes. German thought it would be a good opportunity to talk rifles.

"I have a .22 Cooey for shooting grouse."

"Single-shot?" Shearing questioned.

"Yeah, I'd really like to have one of those pump action ones. That way, I could take a couple of shots at once if I had to."

"I've got one," Shearing proudly claimed. "A .22 Remington. It is pretty accurate and good for hunting deer. It's my dad's rifle and has hardly been used that

I know of." Sounding like he was almost trying to sell the rifle.

When they arrived in the Dawson Creek detachment, the two of them walked in the back door. Standing at the desk was Sgt. Eastham, who German greeted with a smile as he introduced Shearing to him. Shearing's eyes went wide with fear, as Eastham's name had been all over the media as the lead detective on the Bentley Johnson murder case. A different officer escorted Shearing to the interview room while German and Eastham exchanged information about him.

The most crucial thing German could tell Eastham about Shearing was that he always looked down when confronted about a crime he was guilty of. After mentioning the rifle information that he discovered during their drive there, Eastham was ready to start the interview.

PART II

10

A CRACK IN MY SOUL

David Shearing Arrest Photo - Dawson Creek 1983

Before entering the interview room, it was vitally important for Sgt. Eastham to know precisely how he was going to conduct the interrogation, and what questions he wanted to ask Shearing. Eastham had seen plenty of cases dismissed or thrown out of court for the smallest of mistakes, and he didn't want Shearing to end up out on the streets to kill again.

Eastham also knew that they had been working this case for about 15 months now and only had circumstantial evidence. They would need more, a lot more, and if this interview went how they wanted it to go, they would have it. He had gone over the procedure in his head, trying to prepare for everything that could happen. He had to be relaxed yet professional. He would have to be assertive yet passive. He would have to create the perfect balance with Shearing to intimidate him enough into talking but not enough to ask for a lawyer.

Today was Saturday, so the courts were closed, and all the legal aid lawyers were off. So if they played their cards right, they would have about 48 hours to complete the job. He was finally primed and ready. It was time to go to work.

Eastham entered the interview room where Shearing had been seated for a while now across from Detective Ken Leibel. It would be essential to start the interview with good things in life, such as God or Shearing's mother. While they talked about these things, avoiding the crimes, the detectives could look for any weaknesses in their suspect.

Shearing was seated in an old creaky wooden chair, with both of his legs and arms crossed. He was smoking a cigarette, and by the smell of the room, already had a few before Eastham walked in. Leibel was sitting with his chair leaning against the wall, saying nothing.

When Eastham first opened the door, his eyes caught Leibel's, and they both nodded towards each other. While doing this, he could see Shearing moving in his chair to face Eastham. Just then, Eastham turned to look Shearing in the eyes, reached out his hand, and said, "Hi Dave." Shearing stood up, and the two men shook hands firmly. The contest between who would be in charge had now begun.

"You can call me Mike." He continued, "You've met Detective Ken Leibel?" Shearing nodded his head yes as he sat back into his chair. "We're detectives from Kamloops." Eastham then showed Shearing his badge and identification card and then sat down in a third chair beside Leibel.

Eastham noticed Shearing's body beginning to tighten up, and his lips pinched tightly together. He knew he needed to relax Shearing, so he started with some light talk by asking him some basic information.

"Now, Dave, I can really be forgetful sometimes.

I am not very bright, and I tend to forget things a lot. So I'm going to write down our conversation, and Kenny here is going to help me. You don't mind, do you?"

Shearing shook his head to say no.

"What is your full name?"

"David William Shearing."

Back in the eighties, the detectives would usually use a cassette tape recorder to keep a record of everything that went on in the interview room, but in this case, Eastham didn't want to. For one reason, it might scare Shearing, who didn't know the real reason he was there. Secondly, he knew lawyers liked to use the recording to try and find any minor detail they could to get the case dismissed.

"When exactly where you born?"

"Uh, April 10, 1959."

"How long have you been around Tumbler Ridge?"

"Since about the 24th of July."

"Have you got a job in town down there?"

"I did have one there up until about two weeks ago. I was working for Sun Country Construction, putting up forms for basements."

"Alright, Dave, tell me a little more about yourself."

"What do you want to know?"

"Well, tell me about your parents. Where are your parents?"

Finally, with that question, Shearing uncrossed his arms and adjusted his seating to where he appeared more relaxed. "Dad died of cancer last spring." He said with a quiet, soft-spoken tone.

"What about your mother, David. Where is she?"

"My mother still lives in Clearwater. She's been in an old folks' home for some time, and she's not coming out of there, I don't think."

"Any brothers or sisters?"

"One of each. My sister and I don't get along so good. We haven't talked since I left Clearwater. And my brother Greg, we get along pretty good." *(At the time of the interview, Greg was 37-years old and had recently become unemployed)* Shearing, with some pride in his tone, added, "Greg was a sheriff."

"What about you, what kinds of things have you done?"

Shearing lit another cigarette and began to list his accomplishments. "I completed Grade 12 in high school." And he proudly said, "and finished college for heavy-duty mechanics." *(which was a 6-month course).* He continued by listing off some of the construction jobs he had done as well.

"You've done quite a few things in your time, Dave? You must be a real handyman outside?"

"Yeah, I know a lot of stuff."

"Have you had any problems with the law?"

Shearling lit another cigarette and started to spread his legs apart before answering. "Well, there's been a couple of problems, I don't have much money, so I've got to get by." He then mentioned he had been involved with some theft of construction tools and possession of stolen property but figured he would get off with a simple slap on the wrist for that. "I was just being stupid. Some of it was just me, but I had some help from the crowd that I was hanging out with. Not a great crowd, I guess for that sort of thing."

"Ever been to jail?"

"A couple of times in Clearwater, just overnight."

"So, Dave, when were you going to head back to Clearwater to see your mum again?"

"Well, I'd like to go back for Christmas, but I couldn't stay. There isn't much work there, and I kind of like it up here in Tumbler Ridge."

"Do you have a car?"

"A couple of different ones. I just put a new cab on this '72 Ford four by four, but I still need a passenger-side door and some fenders."

This statement got Eastham's attention, as the Bentley's truck had its bumper removed from it, and the passenger-side door had a bullet hole through it. Could he have been trying to fix up the Bentley truck before burning it?

Shearing went on talking about his vehicles. "I've got another Ford, a '75 that I drive right now. I've had a couple of other cars, like a 1965 Chevy Bel-Air. That was my first, and it was all right. I also had a '68 Chevy and a GMC pickup truck."

"Who did you hang out with back in Clearwater?"

"Well, I got along with pretty much everybody. My best bud is probably Allan Smith. I've known him my whole life, but I haven't seen him in about two years."

"Anyone else?"

"Well, let's say that if I walked into a bar in Clearwater, I'd know somebody."

"How about close friends, there's your friend Allan, and?"

"All my friends are close."

"So, what do you like to do in your spare time? Got any hobbies?"

"Well, I like to play guitar. Had to learn that on my own, but it was something I wanted to learn for a long time. I work on my trucks all the time, you know. I like fishing and…"

Eastham interrupts, "And hunting?"

"No," Shearing answered quickly.

"Do you have any firearms?"

"No, I don't have any guns." Then there was a long silence before he finished, "I'm not much of a hunter – just fishing. I spent a lot of time down at the Clearwater River. I like it down there. Best damn trout fishing I've ever seen though was in Dreyfells Lake. I was there this spring."

"I've fished a few times, caught a couple of big ones in my days. Takes a lot of patience." Eastham replied, trying to keep the friendly conversation going.

Shearing sat up straight. "Yeah, patience is a lot of the game. That and a good lure, you have to have the right lure for the water conditions."

"Ever married?"

"Nah."

"Any sweethearts? Girlfriends?"

"Well, there was this one girl in Kamloops, Janet Duncan, she's about 20. I'm terrible with numbers and ages."

"How about names?"

"Well, I'm good with faces, not so much with names," Shearing added while starting to laugh.

"Who knows about you, David? Who do you talk with?"

"You know you guys know more about me than anyone. Except maybe my mother or my brother, and maybe Al."

Eastham then started to explain more. "We want to get to know you, Dave. We want to understand you. The more you tell us, the more we'll understand you. We're doing pretty good right now, don't you think?"

Shearing got a weird look on his face before replying, "It's pretty good."

"It looks like you hit the booze pretty good last night, do you like to drink?"

"Well, lately, yeah, beer mostly."

"Any favorites?"

"Well, probably Budweiser."

"Any liquor?"

"If any, probably rye. Silver Tassel or Canadian Club."

"How about drugs?"

"Haven't done much since high school. I tried acid once and didn't like it. It kind of made me… Well, nothing really. I was just scared to get into stuff like that. Mostly pot back then."

"What about prescription drugs? Have you been taking any medication?"

"No, nothing like that. I don't like taking those kinds of drugs. Don't take them unless I really have to. Like two months ago or so, I was hitting it pretty hard and fell into a fire pit. Stupid really. Burned my back and arm. That was just stupid."

Shearing then continued by telling them about an accident that he had. "This pickup was kind of spinning around and hit my truck. My legs smashed into the dash, and I fractured my pelvis. I don't drink and drive anymore."

Leibel broke his silence and asked. "Was there anybody else in the truck with you?"

"Robert Cliff was there with me."

"Ever been to a psychiatrist?" Eastham came back at him.

"Well, no!" Shearing responded both with surprise, and he had a look on his face as if to say only 'weirdos' do that.

"There's nothing wrong with seeing a psychiatrist, you know. Policemen do it all the time. We have a lot of problems ourselves. Alcoholism, depression, I've seen both of these in my 22 years of policing." Eastham snapped back.

Shearing relaxed a bit. "I guess I thought of seeing a hypnotherapist once to try and quit smoking, but I never ended up doing that, as you can tell. I'd like to quit by the end of the year, but I have a ways to go before then."

Eastham suddenly turned serious again. "Do you know what we're doing here, Dave? Considering the distance that we came, we must be here for a good reason."

Shearing was surprised by the question and sudden change of tone. He started to look down towards his feet. "No, I'm not sure." He answered. "I don't have anything to hide, you know I'm an honest guy."

"We're honest too, David. We don't tell lies, but then, we won't tell you everything we know either. We have a job to do, we're professionals, and were good at what we do. We aren't going to threaten you. We aren't going to beat you, but we won't make promises either. We can't do anything for you. We're always fair. We won't bring any heavies down on you. I know you're no dummy. You've got the same education as me."

"Really!" Shearing replied with a surprise in his voice.

"It means that you don't have to talk unless you want to. It means nobody can make you talk to us." Eastham let the room go tired for a moment before he started up again. "You understand that at any time you want a lawyer, you just say so. If you don't want to answer our questions, you don't have to. Do you understand?"

"Yeah."

"If a lawyer was here right now, he'd tell you to not say anything if you are guilty. He'd tell you to just shut your mouth and not talk to the cops. He says that for a reason, you know?"

"Yes," Shearing said while he nodded his head yes.

"All right, I just wanted to warn you and make

sure you understand. It's important that you know where you are coming from. I want to be honest with you. We're always honest and straight forward."

Shearing just nodded his head as if to agree with what Eastham had been saying again.

"Any time you want to leave, you can. We are going to be talking to you about a lot of criminal things, and I want you to know that that warning applies to all of it. You know you can call a lawyer at any time, and we can't make you any promises. We aren't going to threaten you in any way. Understand?"

"Yeah."

"Any time we're talking, you can get up and leave, okay?"

"Okay."

"We're detectives, GIS - General Investigation Section. We assist several different detachments of the RCMP in the Southern Interior, such as Kamloops, Williams Lake, Merritt, and Clearwater. We're professionals, and we're very good at what we do."

Shearing then asked a surreal question. "Are you guys investigating the Johnson/Bentley murders?"

Again, Eastham let the room go silent for a minute before continuing, "Did anyone talk to you about it last year?"

"Yeah, some cop talked to me about it briefly before, sometime last year."

"A uniformed officer? Or plainclothes?"

"Uh-huh. Uniformed."

"Do you know Trophy Mountain?"

Shearing nodded, yes.

"How about Battle Mountain?"

Shearing continued to nod his head.

"You know that's where we found the truck, camper, and car?"

"Yeah."

"You know we have a lot of members in Clearwater. We know a lot more about you than you think. Everyone wants to help us, even the shit rats. We're getting anonymous calls, a lot of those. Everyone wants to help."

Eastham again let the room go silent for a minute before continuing. "We've been looking under all kinds of rocks. Getting stolen property, drugs, money. Bikers are calling in with all the information they can give us. Bikers!"

This revelation made Shearing look up finally.

"I want to see if you are an honest guy. I'm going to start back a couple of years ago and see what you will do. Remember, you can leave at any time."

Shearing nodded, yes.

"We discovered that a kid was killed that summer on Wells Gray Road. It was a hit and run, or criminal negligence, or whatever. The guy didn't stop. I know all about it; otherwise, I wouldn't be up here in Dawson Creek on a weekend."

There was noticeable relief in Shearing's body, as he probably thought the hit and run was why they were there, not the Johnson/Bentley murders. "I know."

"What happened, Dave?" Eastham asked as he leaned forward on the desk to get his face closer to Shearing's. "Tell me what happened."

"I was driving," Shearing admitted. "I guess you knew that."

"Which way were you going?"

Shearing took a little while, probably to try and remember what happened that night.

"Well, I was driving home, going up the top of the hill, going about 45 or 50 miles an hour. I took my foot off the gas."

"Then what happened?"

"I was scared shitless. I'd been drinking. I knew he was dead."

"How did you know?"

"The whole car ran over him. My whole car bounced; I mean really bounced! He had to be dead instantly."

"Who was with you?"

"You know who was with me." Shearing snapped back.

"Hey, you won't be getting any answers from me, David."

"But I don't want to involve the guy."

"Well, that's up to you." Just then, Eastham sat back in his chair.

"All right, well, you already know it was Doug Elliot."

Without addressing the name Shearing just shared, Eastham continued questioning, "Then what did you do?"

"Well, we were scared to go to the police."

"Why?"

"Cause I had a few drinks. I hadn't been drinking that much, I mean, I could still drive, but I thought the cops would think that I didn't see the body and didn't try to stop. I just didn't have time. We drove into a turn-off and up the road a bit. We were confused. I didn't know what to do."

Shearing paused for a moment before he started up again. "We drove around, but there was a piece of chrome under by the door, dragging along the road. I stopped to pull that off." Shearing suddenly stopped talking again. "Shit, what did I do then? Well, we talked about it for a bit, then we agreed that we shouldn't tell the police about it. I was really scared and confused. I drove Doug home, and I went home shortly after." Shearing then looked at Eastham, "I would imagine you want to ask me more questions about that?"

"Who was the guy you ran over?"

"Dave Carter."

"Did you know him?"

"Yes."

"How did it make you feel?"

"Really confused. I was sad. Well, not sad, I don't know what. I was upset."

"Has it changed your life?"

"I don't know."

"Have you had a tough time living with that?"

Shearing let out a big sigh, "Yeah. I've thought about it."

"Have you had nightmares?"

"No nightmares, but I think about it."

"How many people know?"

"I don't know. I thought it was just Doug and I."

"Well, I'm going to tell you it's no big secret. A lot of people know, except the cops, of course."

"Golly."

"How do you feel now?"

"The shits."

"Well, you've told me and Ken, does that mean anything to you?"

"Yeah, but I'm not sure what."

"Well, a lot of people feel, well, you told me. Do

you think that you might want to write down what happened that night in your own words?"

"I guess so."

Eastham then slid a pad of paper and a pen across the table to Shearing. "Do you want a coffee?"

"Yeah," Shearing mumbled.

Eastham got up from his chair and headed to the door, "Let's get one thing straight," he stopped and turned back to face Shearing, "I'm not giving you anything. I'm getting you a coffee because we were going to have one. What do you want in it?"

"Two sugars."

Eastham left to get the coffees and take a bit of a break. When he came back into the interrogation room with the three coffees in his hand, he was shocked to see that Shearing was crying as he was writing out his statement. He placed the coffees on the table, one in front of Shearing, and didn't mention the crying.

"Having some troubles?" Eastham said as he sat back down into his chair.

"No," Shearing answered slowly, still sniffling away and writing.

Eastham sat and sipped his coffee for a while before leaving the room again. This time for a bathroom break. When he returned to the room, Shearing had his head resting in his left hand, elbow on the table, still writing, sobbing, and taking puffs from his burning cigarette.

Shearing adjusted his chair, sat up, and said, "My stomach is hungry."

"What?"

"My stomach, can't you hear it growling like that?"

Eastham shook his head, "No, sorry."

Shearing continued to write his statement for about 50 minutes before talking again, "Do you have a tissue?"

"Guess what I have in my back pocket?" Eastham replied with a smile as he pulled out a packet of tissues and handed it to Shearing. Shearing then blew his nose a few times, threw away the tissue, then lit another cigarette.

"Jesus, kid. Do you ever smoke?"

Shearing finished blowing his nose and wiping his eyes, "Well, half of them are yours."

Both Eastham and Shearing smiled and chuckled lightly.

After another short silence, Eastham asked, "How are you getting along there?"

"Getting there, I guess. I don't know how detailed you want it."

"It's your statement, not mine. You put down what you think you should put down."

Shearing ripped the first two pages off the paper

pad and numbered them on the top right of the pages and handed them to Eastham. "Well, I've described that night anyway, I think."

"Do you want to sign it, or not? It really doesn't matter."

Shearing signed the bottom of the page, along with Eastham and Leiber, and they put the time at 6:39 p.m. "What happens now?" Shearing asked as if he was ready to leave.

"We'll have to discuss this. Okay, David. You understand everything we've done. I told you when we started that we know a lot about you. We wouldn't be here, especially on a weekend, unless there was a good reason. When we started, we gave you a warning, anything you say can be used as evidence on everything. I also told you we were investigating the Johnson and Bentley murders, and this is where it all stems from. The warning we gave you still stands. As long as you realize that?"

Shearing nodded his head in the affirmative again.

"First, I want to go over this statement."

Eastham slowly read over the statement, only stopping when he needed to clarify some of the words that Shearing had written sloppily or misspelled. "So, this is basically it?"

"Yes, as I remember it."

"Bet that feels good to get that off your shoulders? How do you feel?"

"Pretty tired."

"Have you ever written a statement for the police before?"

"No."

"Well, I guess there's a first time for everything, heh?"

They both laughed.

Eastham asked, "Do you have any questions?"

"I'd like to know what happens next."

"At this point, we'd have to take it up with the prosecutor."

"Am I going to jail?"

"I don't know. It could be criminal negligence or hit and run. My job is to collect the evidence and take it to the prosecutor. The judge then decides what will happen. Both charges are very serious. I don't know which you'll be charged with. It's not up to us."

"What's going to happen to Doug?"

"Again, that's up to the prosecutor. The passenger doesn't have any control of the gas or brake. You know what happened. You did it, you're the one, in your mind. What happens, happens. All things will work out in the end. It's fate. Do you believe in God, David?"

"No," Shearing answered quietly.

"How about your mum?"

"Not really."

"She's an honest person who believes in principles?"

"I believe in principles."

"How do you think this will affect your mother, David?"

"I don't know, she'll worry."

"But she knows you, Dave, a mother knows. She taught you right from wrong. We are taught responsibility. She knows you understand what you did was wrong. She knows you'll take responsibility. That makes you a good person. It's not the people like you we worry about, David. It's the people who don't know they did something wrong, or who don't want to take responsibility for it. I did a profile on you, David. Basically you were pretty quiet up until 1980."

"Yes," Shearing responded while looking towards the floor.

"Two things changed your life, David. One was the death of your father."

Shearing mumble another yes.

"You know, cops go to shrinks for a number of different reasons: stress, alcoholism. We're not unlike anyone else. We did a background on you. We know you have fights. We know someone stabbed you in the chin. We know about the guy you threw out the window, leaving him without the use of his thumb.

We know a lot about you, you know that, and you know what we are here for."

"You knew that I had all the details of the hit and run?" Shearing asked with a surprise in his voice.

"Yeah."

"Did you talk to Doug?"

"I don't tell lies, David."

"Is that the answer?"

"Ah, but David! Like a lawyer, you should never ask a question you don't know the answer to."

Shearing let out a big sigh and lit another cigarette.

"David, what do you think about the Johnson and Bentley murders? What do you think about them being killed in your front yard, so to speak?"

"Well, it was pretty bad for the community."

"Do you know where the car was found?"

"Yeah."

"You know where the truck was found?"

"Yeah."

"You also know where they were killed?"

"Bear Creek." *(At this particular time, nobody in the RCMP actually knew where the family had been murdered)*

"I think I need to speak to a lawyer now." Shearing blurted out.

"David, I think you need a lawyer," Eastham answered. "But I want you to listen to me for a minute.

You don't need to talk; you just need to listen to me. But first I'm going to get some coffee. You guys want another mug?" Everyone answered yes, so Eastham got up, grabbed the empty mugs, and left the room.

(Technically, Shearing never actually asked for a lawyer. He just suggested that he might need one. Therefore, it allowed the detectives an opportunity to keep him talking. Remember, Shearing could have gotten up and left any time unless they arrested him on the hit and run charges.)

By the time Eastham returned to the room with fresh coffee, both Shearing and Leibel had left the room to use the bathroom and stretch their legs. He sat in his chair and started to sip on his coffee, and about 10 minutes later, they walked back into the room. "Just had to check the fluids," Leibel said.

After the two men were seated, Eastham leaned in towards Shearing and started to speak, "David, stupid things happen sometimes. We all do stupid things. It was stupid, David, but I don't know what triggered you to do it. I know it happened. I just don't know why it happened. You do need a lawyer, David; there's no question about it, you need one. But I know what happened, and so do you. The difference is, you know all the details, and I don't."

Shearing tucked his chin into his chest, crossed his arms, and his lip started to quiver slightly.

"If you want to cry, okay, I want to cry too. It's a delicate subject, David. We have to do it sometimes. We don't like it any better than you do. You know that we know. It's changed you, David. You've been boozing it pretty heavy since then. I know you've been trying to put it in the back of your mind."

Shearing's body began to tremble some now.

"I know you want to tell us about it. I know that you do. You just don't know how to right now, and I understand. You don't understand why you did it, and I know you think about it." Eastham continued. "Don't make me involve your mother. I don't want to go and search her place, or your brother's place. I know what happened, and I know it was something that got right out of hand."

Shearing began to cry loud enough that Eastham had to raise his voice.

"I know you're scared, David. There's a lot of pressure on you about this. Most of that pressure is from yourself. You don't have to talk to us, but you want to tell me. You already told me about Doug Carter. You wrote it down, and we discussed it."

Shearing now had his eyes covered with one of his hands, and his mouth with the other hand.

"You knew we'd come for you, didn't you, David?"

"Yeah." Shearing blurted out between sobs.

"Every time you saw a police car, you wondered when we were coming."

Shearing nodded, yes.

"It isn't easy, David; you can't just close your eyes and hope we'll all go away. We won't. We've been going through this for the past 15 months too." Pushing on, Eastham said, "I know that you aren't that kind of person, David. That's why you'll have to explain it. We've got to do this. I don't like it, but we've got to. When I told you that we were from Kamloops, you knew why we were here, didn't you?"

Shearing nodded again.

"There are two ways to do this, David. You could write it out, or we could tape this. You're shaking, though, David. You're upset. I don't think that you could write it. I might be able to write it, or we could tape it. I know you want to help us, David. I know you want to tell us what happened."

The room went silent for a few minutes. Eastham was waiting for Shearing to say something.

"I know you're scared, David, and I know that you're worried about us. You're scared because of what you've done."

All of a sudden, Shearing blurted out loudly, "I could fucking shoot myself! Just go get me your fucking gun and leave me alone with it for a few minutes. I'll take care of everything."

"We don't want you to do that. Your life is important, regardless of what you did. Look, we all make mistakes, and life is quite indifferent about them. The world isn't going to crash to a halt because David Shearing made a mistake. If I had to start all over again every time I made a mistake, I'm not sure where I'd be. Probably still learning to walk. Mistakes are what make us learn. Do you want to do this question and answer style, or would you rather just do this by yourself?"

"I don't know," Shearing answered.

"David, when did you first see the Johnson and Bentley family?"

Shearing said nothing.

"Where did you first see them?"

"Shit, what fucking life?" Shearing shouted out.

"You have a life, David."

"Not anymore, I don't." Shearing looked directly into Eastham's eyes for the first time.

"Your life is important, Dave. Important to you and your family. Don't think for one minute it's not. We're going to go through this together, Dave. I told you I was going to be fair, and I don't lie."

Just then, Eastham reached his hand out across the table and offered it to Shearing, who hesitated for a moment before grabbing hold of it.

"All right, will you tell me about it now?"

"I don't know."

"You know it's going to come out. I know it. I can't tell you to do anything. It's your decision, but we both know you have to tell me. Did you ever think about turning yourself over to the police?"

"No."

"Why not?"

"Don't know."

"What is done is done, David. You can't bring back six lives no matter what. I know you're an honest person. I know you've been drinking. It's not easy to forget something like that. You won't forget. Sometimes people do things, and they don't know why – crimes of passion, or things that just get out of hand. You can't keep hiding from this, David. It's far too late for that now. Do you think you need help?"

"Yeah." Shearing quickly answered.

"Do you know what made you do it, Dave?"

"No."

"Can you remember it very well?"

"Yeah."

"You poor bugger. Let's do it, Dave. It's tough for you, and it's tough for me. Where did you first see the Johnson and Bentley family?"

"Bear Creek."

"Do you remember what day it was when you first approached them? Daytime? Nighttime?"

"Oh God," Shearing screamed out.

"It's difficult for us, Dave. Will you help us out?

You know you're going to tell us, and I know you will too. I know it's hard for you, trying to figure out how you're going to tell us."

"It ain't easy," Shearing said in between his sobs.

"There is no easy way," Leibel added. "You saw them. What time of the day was it, David?"

"I gotta think for a while," Shearing exclaimed. He sat, saying nothing, looking like he was deep in thought. "What happens if I tell you?"

"Well, you will be charged with murder. You'll be in custody, and we will obviously have to have you checked out by a psychiatrist to see why you did it."

Shearing agreed by nodding his head again.

"Where's the gun, David?"

"At the ranch."

"Is it a pump?"

"Yes."

"And the boat and motor?"

"At the ranch."

"Where on the ranch, David?"

"I can draw you a map."

Eastham gave Shearing a piece of paper and a pen. While Shearing drew the map, he explained all the details to the detectives.

"Is the boat under anything, or concealed?" Leibel asked.

"Yes, it's under some bushes."

"Where's the equipment that came with the boat? The gas tank, and life jackets?"

"Underneath it." Shearing finished the drawing and signed at the bottom of the map.

Eastham left the room to get more coffee. This time he was going for the whole jug, as it would take all night to get through all the details of the murders. When he came back into the room, Leibel had Shearing drawing another map.

"All right," Shearing started talking, "This is where they were."

"Where did you come in? The main gate?"

"No, the fence over here." He pointed at a place on the map.

"I came in the campsite through these bushes over here."

"Who did you shoot first?"

"I don't remember."

"These four over here?" Eastham pointed on the map. Shearing nodded, yes. *(Four circles represented the adults in the camp, sitting around the fire)*

Shearing had approached from behind the truck and fired from a position between it and the tent. The tent was just slightly right to the camper. "Then I shot the two in the tent," Shearing said while pointing at the map.

"What then."

"I put them in the car. The adults I put in the back seat, the two girls I put in the trunk."

"Then?"

"I drove the car down to the clearing and parked it there. I then went back and got the truck and parked it there too."

"When does the bullet hole in the truck show up?"

"What?" Shearing asked.

"The bullet hole in the passenger side door. It wasn't done with a .22."

"It wasn't?"

"How many guns did you have?"

"Just the one."

"This was at nighttime that you drove the vehicles?"

"Yeah, well, yes."

"You took the truck to the bare clearing there?"

"Yeah, down there." Shearing tried to show where he parked them, but it was outside of the area of the map he had drawn.

"Do you need another map?"

Shearing grabbed another piece of paper and started drawing a continuation of his map.

"Do you feel like having something to eat?"

"I don't know," Shearing answered while still drawing his new map. "I parked the vehicles here." He stopped drawing and pointed out the spot.

"How far was it from there?"

"About three or four hundred feet."

"How long did you leave the vehicles there?"

"I left them there. I think it was the next day I came down and started sorting through the tools and stuff. I wanted to keep the key for the camper. I don't know why. I'm not sure if it was that day or another day I drove the car up to Battle Mountain."

"Okay, what tools did you keep?"

"A plastic sort of tray of wrenches and stuff."

"Like what?"

"Well, wrenches and pliers. A bunch of tools."

"Where are these now?"

"Probably, some might be in the shed by my house."

"What color was the plastic tray?"

"A bright color. Orange, I think."

"What else was there?"

Shearing went quiet and started to think. Then he began to write down some items on his map. It was vital for Eastham to get as much detail of the things Shearing had taken so that he could get a search warrant for Shearing's house and shed.

"What else do you have at your house or ranch?"

"The camera."

"Where is it?"

"The house."

"What about the film?"

"I tossed it away."
"Where did you throw it?"
"In the camper, I think."
"What else is there?"
"I don't remember."
"Fishing equipment?"
"Didn't keep it."
"Spare tire?"

Shearing had to think for a minute. "Now what the hell did I do with that?" he asked out loud. "It still may be down at the boat."

"Anything else that you can think of?"
"Not really."
"Do you want to do us a map of Battle Mountain, then Trophy Mountain, where the vehicles ended up?"

Shearing nodded yes and started to draw the fourth map.

"All right, insofar as the car is concerned, what did you do?"

"I stopped and walked over to the area. I wanted to see if I could get it there. I decided it would make it and went back to drive it in there."

"What else did you do?"
"I had to move some logs and a couple of rocks."
"Did you have anything when you went in there?"
"A flashlight."

"How about an ax?"
"I might have, but I don't think so."
"Did you chop anything? Any trees?"
"I don't remember." *(A tree was cut down to put the car where it was burned)*
"Then what?"
"I drove it in."
"Did you get stuck?"
"Yeah, on some logs."
"Then?"
"I poured some gas inside the car."
"Did it explode when you lit it?"
"You mean, right away? Well, it went 'whomp.'"
"What did you do with the keys?"
"Jesus, I don't know."
"Did you leave any door open?"
"Yeah, I think I left the drivers-side open."
"Okay, so you're there. You get stuck and get out of your car. You open the trunk, and where was the gas?"
"I don't know."
"Where did you put it first?"
"In the front."
"How did you light it up?"
"A piece of paper, or birch bark."
"It would have been pretty dark at the time, heh?"
"Yeah."
"After you lit the car on fire, where did you go?"

Shearing pointed at a spot on the road.

"Then what happened?"

"I watched it burn for a while, then headed back."

"All right, how about Trophy Mountain? Do you want to mark down what happened to the truck and camper?"

Shearing nodded again, then started to draw out a new map, this one of Trophy Mountain. He then explained how he burned the truck with a full jerry can of gas. He watched it burn for a while before he headed back home.

"Were you drinking when you did this?"

"No."

"What about the camper? What do you remember about the camper? Was there anything else that you took from the camper to Tumbler Ridge?"

"There's the tools in my truck."

"No. In Tumbler Ridge."

"That's what I meant. Did you mean my cabin?"

"Yes."

"No."

"Where's the gun?"

"In the rack at my house, in the front room."

"What kind of a gun is it?"

"An old .22 pump action." *(The detectives now had enough to draw up a search warrant for all of Shearing's residences and vehicles)*

"Now, you can either write out a statement, like

you did the other one, or you can talk, and I'll write everything down?"

"All right, sure."

Eastham grabbed a pen and paper. "All right, don't go too fast."

Shearing went through the series of events from beginning to end.

SHEARING'S STORY ABOUT WHAT HAPPENED THAT NIGHT

Shearing spotted the truck and camper one night in August, on his way home from work. That same evening, he decided he would go for a walk, and somehow found himself at the campsite where he'd spotted the campers earlier. He moved around in the bush until he found a spot that looked down over the camper.

Shearing watched the campers for a short while until he was spooked when he thought one of them spotted him. He quickly got away, running across a field and hiding in some shrubs. He waited there for about 15 minutes just in case he had been followed. Once he was sure that nobody had followed him, he walked back home.

The next night he went back. This time he had a .22 rifle. He followed the same paths; only this time, instead of hiding and watching from the bush, he walked right out into the campsite and started firing his weapon. When the four people by the fire pit were down, he went to the tent, crouched down, and shot the two girls. He loaded the bodies into the car, placing the four adults in the back seat, and the girls into the trunk.

Shearing collected all of the family's possessions, which had been lying around the campsite, and threw them into the back of the camper. He moved both the car and truck with camper a couple of hundred feet away, into the clearing of the field he had run through the night before.

The next day when he returned, he rummaged through the car and removed everything he wanted to keep. He then drove the car up to Battle Mountain and lit it on fire. Two days later, he went and got the truck and drove it to Trophy Mountain. But when it got stuck in the mud, he parked it and torched it where it was.

Shearing claimed that he just stalked the family of six for a couple of nights before shooting them, loaded their bodies in the car, stole some property, drove the vehicles into the night, and torched both the vehicles and the bodies.

But there was much more to the story of what he did that night.

11

SLEEPING WITH THE ENEMY

"And now sleep refuses to come. Not only for me, but for a man whose tension, hour by hour seems to be rising closer to the surface."

Sgt. Mike Eastham

Eastham now had to make arrangements to have them all flown to Clearwater so that Shearing could re-enact the crime. He also had to share all of the information they had on the case with the prosecutor, Bob Hunter, in Kamloops. Hunter would draw up the arrest warrants charging Shearing with six counts of second-degree murder.

The community of Clearwater came alive with word of the arrest. Shearing's mother, Rose, was living in a nursing home when she heard of her son's arrest. Distraught to think that she could have raised a son who would do such a thing, Rose said, "I hope it's a mistake or a bad dream. It has to come to an end. He's always been a good boy."

But on the other side of the coin, Shearing's neighbor in Clearwater, Clayton Hicks, said, "I'm not surprised he got arrested for the murders. We knew him better than most people around here did, but I can't say anything more because I don't want to mess things up for the cops."

Although most people in Clearwater expressed a state of shock that it was Shearing who was arrested for the murders, a big sigh of relief came from them. After the bodies were discovered so close to the town, people started to arm themselves as they walked around. Nobody would let their children out alone, and women always walked in groups of at least two or three at a time. The backbone of the economy at the park and nearby towns was tourism. And that fell to almost nothing after the murders. All of the parks that would typically be full of campers and travelers were now empty.

After Shearing finished his statement, he was taken to a cell, and Eastham got Constable Ron German and his dog Max to stay with Shearing in his cell that evening. At about 11:30 p.m., German went into the cell where Shearing was being held and got him some towels and blankets for the night.

"Thanks, Ron," Shearing said.

"No problem," German answered as he draped a towel over Shearing's shoulder. "Anything else you need, just let me know."

"Okay, thanks."

Shearing finished cleaning himself up, went back to his cell, and climbed into the bunk. German locked the cell door, grabbed a chair, and slid it in front of Shearing's cell door.

"How long are you going to be staying in Dawson, Ron?"

"Until tomorrow. We just want to make sure that you've got someone here in case there's anything you need."

"Well. I really appreciate it. I guess there'll be

someone with me for a while."

"Probably."

"How long are your transfers for?"

"Pardon?"

"Well, how long are you going to be in Tumbler?"

"About two years. Generally, in a place like Tumbler, you serve two years. After that, you can pretty much pick where you want to go. It cost a lot of money to transfer members. Let's say I found a place where I liked; they'd probably let me stay there as long as I wanted, depending on where it was."

"Do you like Tumbler?"

"It's alright there, but I couldn't see myself staying up there more than two years."

"I like it up there a lot, but I guess I'm going to be seeing the inside of these for a while. Maybe even a padded one."

"You think so?"

"I guess I've got to go into a 30-day psych remand."

"Yeah, they do that for all cases like these."

"I guess I'm going to have to look at black blotches and tell them what I see."

"Yeah, it's a tough job to figure out what's in the mind. Really though, maybe it'll be good for you to go in there and have someone talk to you about what's in your mind. Maybe it'll help you understand yourself a bit more."

"Maybe. What's the chances I can get some of my clothes from the cabin?"

"I'm sure I can make some arrangements to get some of your stuff."

"There's a couple of kit bags there in under the bed and stuff. Those belong to Doug and Willie, but the rest of the stuff is mine."

"All right."

"Could I have a cigarette?" Shearing was allowed to have his cigarettes in the cell, but not a lighter. German had to light a cigarette for him and pass it back to him through the cell.

"I guess being a cop is pretty hard?"

"You could say that. A lot of people don't understand how hard it is without following us around and watching what we go through. I guess after a while you get used to it, and it almost seems normal."

"How long have you been a cop?"

"About seven years. I was in Powell River before I was transferred over to Tumbler. That's actually where I met Mike Eastham."

Shearing covered his eyes, then said. "I've got to stop thinking about this."

"I bet you've got a lot on your mind. Do you want a tissue or something like that?"

"No. I am all right. I bet this will keep the papers happy for a while."

"Yup, so long as they've got their story, and make money, they'll be happy."

"Will my family be notified before it makes the papers?"

"Well, it will be a couple of days before the papers get any word of it. I'm sure you could tell your family on your own. You can probably make any arrangements that you want."

German walked down to the main office and tried to turn the lights off, but was unable to, so he returned to Shearing's cell, who was still sitting up on his bunk.

"Do you like to fish?"

"What?" German sounded surprised.

"Fishing? We talked about hunting before. I was wondering if you fish?"

"Well, not too much, I used to when I had more time."

"There's some good rivers near Tumbler for fly fishing. I used to fish all the time in Clearwater too. I loved fishing." Just then, Shearing couldn't stop the tears from coming down his face, so he started wiping them with his hands. "Shit!" he exclaimed as he laid down on his bunk, with his hands still covering his face. "I guess I won't be as hated as Olson is, I know a lot of people wanted to kill him."

"He's a different kind of person than you, Dave."

"Yeah, but I bet there's a lot of people out there that want to kill me too?"

"Isn't Olson out east now?" German asked just to try and change the subject of people wanting to kill Shearing.

"I think so. They gave him his own trailer and stuff like that. I guess they're not used to having someone like that in cells. I sure hope the cells in Kamloops are better than this."

"Actually, I think they're just like this," German replied. Shearing got up and started walking around the cell again.

"I'm going on my first plane trip tomorrow, down to Kamloops on the police plane. You ever been on it?"

"Yeah, a couple of times, it's a nice aircraft."

Shearing stopped pacing and looked German right in the eyes. "So, what's going to happen to me when I go to court?"

"You mean security-wise?"

Shearing nodded yes and sat back down on the bunk.

"Well, I'm not really sure about that, Dave. There will probably be extra security around the courthouse to make certain that you don't get hurt."

"Will it be open to the public?"

"That's up to the judge, but I'm pretty certain it will be."

"This is going to be tough on my family. I'm not sure how I'm going to tell them."

"Well, you tell them that you did something very wrong, and you've taken responsibility for your actions. You confessed and cooperated because you understand that what you did was really bad."

"I wish it were that easy. What's going to happen to that moose we saw on the highway?"

"Well, if the department of health determines that the meat is salvageable and still good, it gets sent to the old folks' home."

"That's good that they do that."

"Did you know what was going on when I picked you up, David?"

"No, I didn't have a clue." Soon after, Shearing fell asleep.

The next morning, German got Shearing ready for his flight to Kamloops, and then Clearwater. Shearing was going to do a reenactment of the crime for the detectives. Before leaving, he had a short interview with the two detectives, Len Bylo and Gerry Dalen, who would be doing the reenactment with him, before heading out to the plane.

As he was boarding the plane, he stopped, turned around to face German, and said, "Thanks, Ron.

Thanks for staying with me last night." German shook Shearing's hand. "Good luck, David." Shearing got into the plane, and they flew off to Kamloops.

12

MY PAIN'S NOT ASHAMED TO REPEAT ITSELF

"On this great and gloomy mountain, life goes on as usual, and so does death, with the doubts and fears that accompany it. Especially when it is a death that has not been fully explained."

Re-enactment of the Crime

The murders happened in August, the middle of summer when things were hot. It was now winter, and there was snow covering the ground, so things looked different, and it was more challenging for Shearing to spot some of the exact locations. Still, the detectives knew they needed to get as much evidence for the trial as they could. This was a crime without witnesses, and one mainly riding on the confession of Shearing.

Detectives Bylo and Dalen took Shearing to the crime scene in a Ram Charger pickup truck, and Eastham and Leibel followed them in a Plymouth. As they got closer to the murder scene, Bylo asked,

"David, weren't you nervous about someone seeing you here driving around on this road?"

"Well, yes, but it was late at night, eh."

"About what time was it?"

"Almost midnight, at least."

"Did you know where you were going the night before you got rid of the truck and camper?"

"Not really. I'd been there before, but not exactly at that spot."

They headed up to the location on Trophy Mountain, where Shearing told them to stop. Bylo asked, "Dave, can you get out and show us the spot where you drove the truck and camper?"

Shearing got out of the truck. "Yeah, sure." He then pointed out the area where he parked the truck and camper.

"Dave, what was the reason for burning the truck and camper?"

"To get rid of the evidence."

Everyone got back into their vehicles, and they headed out towards the Old Prison Camp on Wells Gray Road. "Is this where you murdered those people, the four adults, and two children?"

"Yes," Shearing replied.

The detectives had Shearing show them where the truck and camper were parked, and they parked their Ram Charger in the same spot. Next, they had Shearing show them where the car was parked, and they parked their Plymouth in the same spot. Shearing told them where the tent was and described where the adults were sitting around a campfire.

"Dave, will you show me where you walked in from the woods the night you shot those people?"

Shearing walked up from behind the Ram Charger (the truck and camper on the night of the murders), demonstrating how he carefully kept out of sight of the campfire.

"How long did you stand there and watch them?"

"A couple of minutes."

"Dave, now show me exactly where the adults were when you shot them?"

"They were all sitting around here," he said as he pointed out where the campfire was. "But I think one of them was standing."

"Which direction were they looking?"

"Their backs were all facing me."

"Dave, do you remember where the men were sitting when you shot them?"

"Not really, I couldn't tell you."

"All right, Dave, where were the girls when you shot them?"

"They were over here in the tent," Shearing said as he walked over to where the tent was standing that night.

"Where were you standing when you shot the girls?"

Shearing knelt down on his knees in the grass and pretended to be holding a rifle in his hands, pointing at what would have been the girls in the tent. *(During this time, many pictures were taken of the demonstrations that Shearing did)*

They ordered Shearing back into the truck and then drove about ten minutes to where he had burned and left the car. Just before they exited the truck, Bylo asked Shearing, "Were all of the people dead before you loaded them in the car?"

"Yeah."

"Now, why did you burn the car and the bodies?"

"I imagine the same reason that I burned the truck and camper, to get rid of the evidence."

"What time of the day was it when you burned the car?"

"It was nighttime, probably about nine or ten o'clock."

They all returned to their vehicles and headed up to where Shearing told them he had hidden the boat. Shearing told them to stop when they got there. They all got out of the truck and followed him over to a section of the woods. Shearing pulled some shrubs away, and the boat appeared.

After that, they headed to Shearing's house, where they parked and went inside. The first thing they spotted was the gun rack hanging in the living room. Right away, Dalen asked, "Would you now show me the gun you used to shoot and kill the families? The Johnson and Bentley families that is."

"It's this one here," Shearing pointed out the rifle that was hanging at the top of the gun rack.

"Are there any bullets like those you used to kill the families?"

"There might be some on the rack there."

"David, you mentioned some tools, where are they?"

"They're over in that shed there."

"Let's go take a look." They all walked over to the shed. After a complete search of the shed, they all piled into the truck and headed back to the Clearwater detachment. Later Shearing was charged with six counts of second-degree murder.

13

FREEDOM COMES WHEN YOU LEARN TO LET GO

Court Drawing of Shearing

The trial was set to start on Monday, April 16, 1984, in the Supreme Court located in Kamloops. Shearing retained lawyer Fred Kaatz from the Mair Jensen Blair law firm, considered one of the best in B.C. Fred Kaatz was a very well-respected defense attorney who had spent several years as an investigator for the RCMP.

A few days before the trial was to start, prosecutor Bob Hunter called all of the detectives who had worked the case into his office. Hunter wanted to commend them all for doing such a great job, collecting the evidence so well that there wasn't a possibility Shearing would get off on any of the charges of murder. However, that wasn't the real reason Hunter called them into his office. He wanted to tell them that the case was not going to go to trial. The defense team led by Fred Kaatz was copping pleas to all six counts of second-degree murder. It would be up to the prosecution to secure a sentence of life without a chance of parole for 25 years. The normal for a case like this was life with possible parole in 15 years, so they still had their work cut out for them.

In Sgt. Eastham's mind, this left some unfinished business. Experience told him there was more to this story. He knew Shearing had not been completely honest and forthcoming with everything that happened that night. It was time to visit Shearing and find out if he would tell him everything.

Eastham went to visit Shearing in jail on the morning of April 16, 1984, before his court appearance.

"How ya feeling, Dave?"

"Well, not bad, I guess considering."

"I'm going to be straight with you, David. You know I've been around for a long time. I've been a cop for 22 years, and you know cops hear a lot of stories. Look, I don't have any reason to think that you lied to me, David, but I got a feeling gnawing in my guts that something else happened that night, and you're not telling me what that is."

Shearing put his head down and pointed his eyes towards his feet. Eastham knew that meant Shearing was hiding something. "You told me once that you might tell me the whole story one day, and I left it at that. Well, David, the day you're sentenced, I'm going to come and collect." Eastham stood and walked to the cell door. "Think about it, David, I'll be back."

Detectives Bylo and Dalen drove up to the courthouse. They had Shearing in the back seat of their unmarked police car. The sidewalks and lawns surrounding the courthouse were covered with reporters. The courtroom was already full, including members of the

Johnson and Bentley families. Extra security was taken to ensure that nobody would try and shoot or attack Shearing while bringing him into the courthouse.

The courtroom went silent as Shearing was brought in. Everyone stood as Justice Harry McKay walked onto the bench. The court clerk stood and read out all of the charges against Shearing. McKay asked how Shearing pleaded. His defense attorney stood and told the court that Shearing would be pleading guilty to all charges. Before McKay could accept the pleas, he would have to ask Shearing himself if he understood the full extent of what he was doing. "You understand that you are admitting fully and unequivocally to having committed the murders charged against you?"

Shearing stood and answered. "Yes."

"And you understand that, as I have already mentioned to counsel, what the possible penalties are?" McKay continued.

"Yes," Shearing replied.

McKay then asked Shearing to be seated before he accepted the pleas of guilty on all six counts. The judge adjourned for the lunch break, and when everyone returned, both the prosecution and defense took turns on presenting their recommendations of what the sentence should be, and their reasons.

The next morning, Tuesday, April 17, 1984, the

court proceedings continued. Judge McKay returned and was going to impose his sentence on Shearing.

"Mr. Shearing, would you please stand." Shearing and his lawyer both stood facing the judge.

"The prisoner has pleaded guilty to six counts of second-degree murder. The facts as they emerge from his statement show the senseless, ruthless, cold-blooded slaughter of six innocent and defenseless victims, a slaughter that devastated three generations of a single-family.

Two of the victims, the grandparents, Mr. and Mrs. Bentley, were enjoying their retirement years. Mr. and Mrs. Johnson were raising a family and in the prime of their life. The other two young girls, one 11 and the other 13, had their whole lives ahead of them. The victims were enjoying a family reunion and a camping trip in one of our wilderness areas when this senseless slaughter occurred. The adults were sitting around a campfire at the end of a no doubt enjoyable day, and the young girls had retired to their tent for the night.

What a tragedy. What a waste, and for what? As best as I am able to judge, the only motive for this mass killing was that the prisoner coveted their possessions. The sentence for second-degree murder is life imprisonment. The only issue before me is as to the period the prisoner must serve before becoming eligible for parole."

The judge went over all of the points that both the defense and prosecutors brought up in court on the previous afternoon, then continued.

"Dealing with the nature of the offenses and the circumstances surrounding their commission, I must, of course, be careful to ensure that I do not treat these murders as though they were first-degree murders, thus requiring a period of ineligibility of 25 years. The crown elected to charge second-degree murder in each case, and I assume that was because of the perceived frailty in the evidence relating to the planning and deliberation as those words have been defined in the jurisprudence on the subject.

Parliament has decreed that sentencing judges may, on conviction for a second-degree murder having regard to the criteria set out in section 671, increase the period of ineligibility for parole from 10 years up to a maximum of 25 years. Obviously, an increase to the maximum of 25 years would be a rare event. I am unaware of it being done in any other case to date. In my view, however, this is an appropriate case for such a drastic action. The enormity of the crimes demands the maximum sentence.

Mr. Shearing, with respect to each of the six counts of murder that you have pleaded guilty, I sentence you to concurrent terms of imprisonment for life without eligibility for parole until you have served 25 years of your sentence."

Shearing was taken to a room at the back of the courthouse, where he and his lawyers had a meeting. At this point, it was safe to assume they were planning how to get Shearing into the general population of whichever prison he would be sent to, so he could do his time comfortably and not caged in solitary confinement.

They also knew Eastham wanted to talk with Shearing about what else happened on the night of the murders. Kaatz knew that Eastham would be writing the parole reports for Shearing and figured it might be better for Shearing to tell him his secrets to get some leniency on those future reports, perhaps.

Kaatz told Shearing that he was free to tell Eastham anything that he wanted to. He reassured Shearing that nothing could be done to him legally either as he was already tried and convicted of the crimes. After Kaatz left, Eastham entered the room to talk with Shearing. As soon as Eastham had a seat, Shearing told him that he would tell him everything.

CONVERSATION BETWEEN EASTHAM AND SHEARING

Shearing started, "I guess I was at the Bear Creek site one of those nights on my way home from work."

Eastham asked, "You remember which night?"

"I think it was Thursday or Friday I saw the family there – a couple of older folks with these two young girls. I guess I got it in my mind that I wanted them. I went back, and I'm not sure if it was that night or the following night. I knew I was going to have to kill those other four to get the girls. I watched them for about 45 minutes, sitting upon this sort of hill, where I'd watched them the nights before. I showed it to you back when we went to the park. When I was there, one of the women saw me."

"Which one?"

"I don't know. It was pretty dark."

"What happened then?"

"Well, she started standing up. And I said, 'Don't move! I got a gun.' Then the younger guy stood up, and I shot him."

"Where did you shoot him, David?"

"I think I hit him in the throat because he was gurgling and making a lot of noise. Then the older guy started running over to the truck, and I shot him next to the passenger-side door. The mother of the girls was running for the tent, and I shot her in the head about halfway between the fire and the tent. Then I headed around to get the older woman, who was trying to get into the camper. I just came up behind her and shot her in the head too. Once they were all dead, I went over to the tent. The girls were in there, kind of sitting up on their elbows. They asked me what all the noise was, and I said there were some bad people out there, and your parents told me to stay back so that they could go get some help. They asked me if it was motorcycle people, and I said, 'Yeah, don't come out. Whatever you do, don't come out.' Then I went back out and had to shoot the young guy."

"Bob Johnson? He's got a name, David!"

"Yeah, Bob Johnson. I'm not good with names. Anyway, I shot him again because he was making all the noise. Then I had to put the bodies in the car."

"That had to be pretty tough."

"It wasn't easy. I had a little blood on my hands. I covered them up with a blanket when I was done, and then went back and cleaned up some of the other stuff. There wasn't too much sitting around, so it didn't take long. I went over to the tent when I was done, and crawled in."

Shearing then described the sexual assault that he had committed against the girls in more detail.

"After I got dressed, I got them to help me take down the tent. They asked where their parents were a couple of times, and I told them they got away to get help. We cleaned up the rest of the site and put most things inside the camper. I guess they believed me as they did everything I said. They didn't see me shoot the parents, so I guess they didn't have any reason not to believe me."

"We got in the car, and I told them to sit in the front beside me."

(How Shearing thought anybody would believe this story is beyond me. First off, when he started shooting the parents at the campsite, I'm sure there would have been screaming from the mother, for instance, when she first spotted Shearing, or from the three other adults when he shot the first woman. So, for Shearing to say that the girls didn't know what was happening outside their tent is ridiculous. Then, for Shearing to go into the tent after all of that and sexually assault the girls? They were 11 and 13 years

old, and they would have known right then that Shearing was a bad man. Add that to the fact that they would have seen the four dead adult bodies piled in the back seat, all bleeding out in the car. And the girls wouldn't realize what was happening? More lies!)

Shearing continued with his story. "We drove back around Wells Gray Road and headed up to the ranch. When I got to where I wanted us to be, I got the girls out of the car and had them set up the tent. I told them that the biker people were still around and looking for them, so they weren't to leave. They were so scared they did everything I told them to."

He then told Eastham that he walked back to the campsite and got the truck and camper and drove it to where he wanted to hide them on the ranch. When he returned to the ranch, he told the girls that he had saved their parents and helped them to getaway. "They really thought that I was their hero." He then told the girls that they shouldn't leave the tent, as there were bears and wolves as well as the bikers out there that would get them. If the bears showed up, he told them that they could hide in the camper. "They were scared shitless, and would do anything I wanted them to, and once they were settled in the tent, I went back home. The next morning Shearing went into work as usual and left the girls there alone. "I brought them bread and milk and stuff, when I came home, I think it was Wednesday night, or maybe it was Thursday from work."

"And you murdered the parents on?"

"I'm pretty sure it was Monday."

"All right."

"That next day, Tuesday, I mean, I came back that night. I came back to see them, and I was still their hero. I told them that I had talked to their parents and that they told me it was safest for them to just stay there with me. They were pretty happy with that story, and they trusted me. We talked a lot at night before they went to sleep, and I had some beer out there with me to drink in the camper. Both the girls slept out in the tent as the younger one had a fear of the camper and was kind of claustrophobic."

On Friday night, Shearing returned to tell them that their parents would meet them at a remote fishing cabin. They left the ranch and began working their way through the dense brush in the dark. "It was raining like hell," Shearing exclaimed. "I tried to light a fire for them because they were really cold and wet, but I couldn't." Shearing then explained how they camped out in the woods, where he covered them with a sheet of plastic that he had brought with them. He also claimed that the two girls slept in one sleeping bag, while he slept in the other.

The next day, he said they continued to travel through the woods until they came to the river. At the river, they turned downstream and went for about a mile until they reached his cabin. There they hung all of their clothing and sleeping bags out to dry. That night they stayed inside the cabin. Again he was in one sleeping bag; the two girls were in the other.

It was now Sunday morning. Shearing said when they got up, he had spotted some prisoners fishing in the river. "My dad was a prison guard, so I wasn't too worried about it," Shearing claimed. Later that day, Don Gordon, a prison guard for the Clearwater Corrections Centre, came up to the cabin door and told Shearing some real mild prisoners were fishing in the river, and he didn't need to be worried about them. Shearing also said that the guard didn't see the girls with him.

"Where were the girls?"

"I hid them behind the door and told them to be quiet. They did everything I said."

After Gordon left and went back to his prisoners, Shearing took the girls and left, heading back to the ranch. "The girls were really slow on the way back. I guess they were really tired from all of the walking that we had been doing. When we got back to the ranch, everything was still set up the way we had left it."

Not too long after they returned, Shearing asked Karen to go for a walk with him to talk about a personal matter. Karen followed him, and once they got out of range from the ranch, they stopped. "I told her that I had to take a piss, so she turned around. I had the .22 stashed there, so when she wasn't looking, I shot her in the back of the head. When I went back to the camp, I had a beer and sat around. When Janet asked where Karen was, I told her that I had tied Karen to a tree. And that night, Janet and I were in the camper. Janet was a virgin and didn't know a lot about sex at all. She didn't know how to do anything, so we just stayed up most of the night and talked about everything. That morning, Tuesday, I think, I asked Janet to come for a walk with me down the trail. She came, and when we got to the spot where I hid the rifle, I asked her to turn around so that I could take a piss. When she did, I shot her in the back of the head and killed her also. I loaded the two bodies in the trunk, then went into the ranch and went to bed."

The next night, Shearing went back to the car and drove it up to Battle Mountain. It had been ten days now that the bodies had laid in the back seat of the car. Shearing wanted to drive the car far into the woods before he burned it, only he got stuck in the mud so badly that he gave up trying and burned it where it sat.

It was now about August 23, and the tourist alert had gone out, which might have been the signal for Shearing to take the truck and camper up the mountain and torch it. "I knew the area pretty well," Shearing explained. "There was a big gully there, and I wanted to drive the truck right off the cliff. That way, nobody would ever find it." The night before, it had rained hard, and the ground had turned to mud. So, when he drove it up to the spot where he wanted it to be, he got stuck again. After trying hard to get the truck out of the rut in the ground, he gave up and lit it on fire. After watching it until the fire took hold, he headed for home.

Eastham got up and left from the meeting with Shearing, knowing that it was all he would get out of him, and he needed to take a long break from hearing about such a horror. He needed some solitude.

After this interview, Detective Leibel went out to check Shearing's cabin. He found a spot where Shearing had carved his initials into the cabin's wooden logs. It said DS + JJ.

There is so much to this story that none of us will ever know. When Eastham brought his findings to other law enforcement members, it wasn't considered credible and would never be used in any way. I think that what Eastham was doing was right. After all, he was just trying to find out what happened that night.

Some say that the trial story was good enough,

and the family members didn't need to know the details to get closure and move on with their lives. This statement is absolutely untrue. I've met many of these family members, old neighbors, teachers of the girls, and friends. There is no such thing as closure when tragic events like this happen. It doesn't end with the trial and conviction. It never ends. What does happen is that all of these people's lives change forever. And after a while, the shock, sadness, and anger fade away enough that they can get up in the mornings, have their coffee, go to work and continue with their lives.

The truth is we don't know precisely what happened the night that Shearing went into the Johnson and Bentley campsite. But knowing that a killer describes his story in a way that is angled to try and make us think he wasn't so bad tells us enough. Shearing told his story in a way to try and make the listeners feel sorry for him.

If you were to return to the old prison site, where the Johnson and Bentley families spent their last night alive, you would find it barricaded with a fence and a large sign that reads "Ministry of the Attorney General – No Trespassing." But over the fence, you can still see the clearing they used to set up their camper and tent. There are still even remnants of the fire pit they used to toast their marshmallows before bedtime. Around the camp, there are still plenty of places to pick fresh berries and mushrooms. Edith Bentley loved to bake Huckleberry pies for not only her family but almost anybody that she knew. The old prison site was the perfect setting to get her Huckleberries.

Through a tiny and now mostly overgrown trail, just over a kilometer away was where the Shearing family ranch is. The house is no longer there. Not even a foundation is visible beyond the fence that surrounds what used to be the house. On that fence, there's another warning posted on a sign telling people that there is no trespassing allowed.

Three years after the trial, during the winter of 1987, the Shearing house burned to the ground. There was never an explanation given or reason why provided. I can say that there was no power hooked up to the house back then, and nobody was living there. Rumor has it that it was torched to the ground by angry people from the town of Clearwater.

Clearwater lived under a dark cloud after the bodies of the Johnsons and Bentleys were discovered there. The town primarily relied on tourists, people that would travel to Wells Gray Park for their vacations. Anglers and hunters always loved that area of the country. But after the murders, the parks sat nearly empty, and nobody wanted to go camping, fishing, or hunting in that area. The town started to run rampant with rumors and stories about the killings.

Did Shearing do it alone? Who helped Shearing clean up the bodies and hide the vehicles? Why did he kill the family? Did someone else hire him to do the murders? Did the police lie about what really happened? Most of these questions are still asked today around town.

During the last few years of writing and researching this book, I received several emails, messages, and phone calls, that all started by saying much the same things to me. Do you know what really happened? Did you talk with "XYZ"? (they would say a name of someone that was out of Clearwater, a friend of Shearing or sometimes even a family member) Do you know what I heard? Do you know what everyone in Clearwater thinks?

My first response was always, "so, are you telling me that you know what really happened on the night of the murders?" I was starting to feel like I was in some detective movie, where there was a big cover-up going on, and the murders weren't what they appeared to be. Some even told me the cops were involved! I was starting to hear the *Mission Impossible* theme play in the back of my mind every time I received a phone call or email about this case.

Remember that Clearwater, B.C., only has about 2,300 residents living in the town. That's small enough where everyone knows everyone's business. In several of these cases, the stories circulate over and over, and I am sure the original story has changed and had all sorts of colorful embellishments added to them.

Could there be some truth to these local stories? Possibly, but we have to be able to see through all of the emotions and look at just the facts. Just because we don't like someone, or think that they behave weird, we can't make them evil and classify them as being involved in a murder.

The story that I heard the most was about David Shearing's mother. She had been placed in an assisted care facility before the murders. After David was arrested, she told several people, in fact, anyone that would listen to her, that she believed David didn't commit the murders. And that the police had the wrong man. She knew David, and in her heart, she knew that he couldn't kill anybody. Later on, after the trial and David was convicted, she still didn't believe it. A mother never wants to believe that her son could brutally kill a family just to steal their possessions. Remember at the time of the trial, he was charged and convicted of second-degree murders for reasons of theft. The sexual assault of the two girls was never mentioned.

Now that David confessed and was convicted, she started saying that David didn't act alone. There was no way he could have gathered all the bodies, put them in the car, burned them, and then burned and hid both vehicles. She now claimed that David had help from his brother Greg. Greg Shearing was a sheriff in Prince George, B.C. for a few years before the murders, but decided to quit being a sheriff after his brother David was arrested and charged with murder.

Many of the messages I received suggested that Greg helped David Shearing with burning the truck and camper and trying to hide the evidence after the fact. Of course, there is no concrete evidence of this, just Clearwater resident's rumors, started by Shearing's mother, who believed it to be true. She was saddened and heartbroken to think she could have had a son who would murder a family of six and sexually assault their two little girls. She prayed hard that he would be found innocent and that it was all a big mistake.

I mentioned these messages to different police officers involved in the case, and none of them found any evidence of such a thing happening. Some officers who knew Greg and spoke with him during this time said Greg hadn't acted out of the ordinary. Sgt. Ron German first met Greg in Chetwynd, BC when he handed over Dave's possessions he recovered from the cabin. At the time, Greg said he didn't believe Shearing did it, but if he did, then he would disown him as a brother and hope they would throw away the key. German detected no suspicion at all during his interaction with Greg.

14

FORENSIC OPTOGRAPHY

As a true-crime writer, I often find myself trying to figure out the truth behind what happened in an unsolved murder. However, I don't do this in the usual armchair detective way. I like to imagine all aspects of the crime, and who would know the answer. Of course, that is always the killer themselves, and quite often the person they are murdering. I say quite often since there are times when the victim doesn't know they are about to be murdered, so, therefore, doesn't always know who the killer is.

If you were being strangled by someone and the whole time they had their hands wrapped around your neck while you were fighting them off, you would lock stares with them until it all went dark. The image of the killer's eyes and face you had stared into until your death would be the last thing you'll ever see. Consequently, like a piece of film in an open box camera that's been exposed to light for a matter of time, that image has been burned into your retinas. Suppose we were able to remove your eyes after you were murdered in such a way. Would it be possible to 'develop' the image left on your eyes, thereby identifying who you saw last?

This concept, referred to as optography, isn't a completely new idea, of course. Many people have wondered about this before I was ever born, and in some cases, they even studied it scientifically. Police investigators in the late 1800s considered it as a possible new tool for investigating murders. One of the earliest known attempts at forensic optography occurred in 1877, when Berlin police photographed the eyes of murder victim Frau von Sabatzky, on the chance that the image would help solve the crime. In 1888, London police officer Walter Dew, who was later known for catching the murderer, Dr. Crippen, recalled optography being attempted on Mary Jane Kelly in what he called a "forlorn hope" of catching her suspected killer, Jack the Ripper. Ripperologist James Stewart-Gordon believed the technique was attempted on Annie Chapman as well.

This technique wasn't just being performed in Europe. America had made attempts as well. But W.C. Ayres, an American physician who assisted

Kühne in his laboratory and translated his papers into English, dismissed the theory that optography on a human eye could yield a usable image for forensic purposes. In an 1881 article in the New York Medical Journal, Ayres stated that his repeated experiments in the field had produced some optogram images. Still, they were not distinct enough to be useful. He declared it "utterly idle to look for the picture of a man's face, or of the surroundings, on the retina of a person who has met with a sudden death, even in the most favorable circumstances."

A rare case of forensic optography being admitted as evidence occurred in late 1924 after German merchant Fritz Angerstein was charged with killing eight members of his family and household staff. Doehne, a professor at the University of Cologne, photographed the retinas of two of the victims. He claimed the technique showed images of Angerstein's face and an ax used to kill the gardener. Angerstein was tried, convicted, and executed, with Doehne's optographic images included as evidence. According to the Sunday Express newspaper, when told of the "incriminating" optograms, Angerstein confessed to the murders.

The most recent research into the use of optography in criminology occurred in 1975 when police in Heidelberg asked Evangelos Alexandridis at the University of Heidelberg to re-evaluate Kühne's experiment findings with modern scientific techniques, knowledge, and equipment. Like Kühne, Alexandridis successfully produced several distinct high-contrast images from the eyes of rabbits. But he negatively assessed the reliability of the technique as a forensic tool.

The idea of forensic optography did come to me as it did to all the previous investigators listed above. Even though it became apparent than this technique was not a reliable way to solve a crime, my mind nevertheless dwelled on it. I still wondered about what the person being killed saw, but also what the murderer was seeing while he was doing the killing.

15

FIGHT FROM THE INSIDE

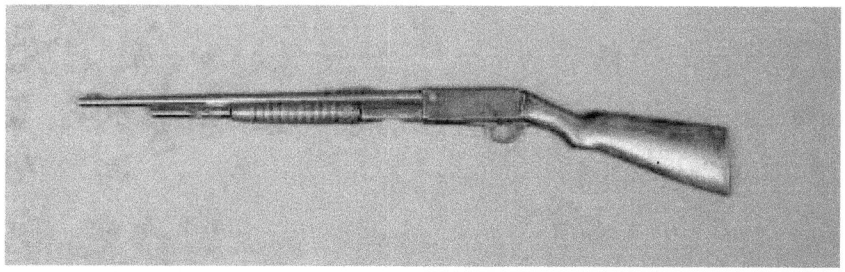

Shearing's .22 Calibre Rifle

Sometime in the 1930s, neuroscience became a widely recognized discipline within science, and the first use of lobotomies was used to try and figure out the abnormal mind. Scientists wanted to know if serial killers were born that way, or was it something that happened as they grew? Whatever the final result would end up being, they couldn't know. But what they did discover was a definite connection between criminal behavior and specific deficits in the brain.

A new study of 1,024 mammal species had determined which animals were the most vicious killers. Out of all species, which one would you guess likes to kill its own kind the most? If you think it's some wild animal such as a tiger or bear, you'd be wrong. Perhaps maybe a pit bull? No, wrong again. The animal most likely to kill its own over seven times that of any other animal is us, the human.

"Our violence operates far outside the bounds of any other species. Human beings kill anything. Slaughter is a defining behavior of our species. We kill all other creatures, and we kill our own. Read today's paper. Read yesterday's or read tomorrow's. The enormous industry of print and broadcast journalism serves predominantly to document our killing. Violence exists in the animal world, of course, but on a far different scale. Carnivores kill for food; we kill our family members, our children, our parents, our spouses, our brothers and sisters, our cousins, and in-laws.

FIGHT FROM THE INSIDE | 155

We kill strangers. We kill people who are different from us, in appearance, beliefs, race, and social status. We kill ourselves in suicide. We kill for advantage and for revenge, we kill for entertainment: The Roman Coliseum, drive-by shootings, bullfights, hunting and fishing, animal roadkill in an instantaneous reflex for sport. We kill friends, rivals, coworkers, and classmates. Children kill children, in school and on the playground. Grandparents, parents, fathers, mothers-all kill and all of them are the targets of killing..."[1]

When looking back through history, we see that humans were killing each other as long ago as our primate days, only we weren't killing each other quite as much back then. Why is that?

Scientists assert that the main reason for our killing nature comes from our brain's basic functioning. It's our consciousness or awareness of ourselves that does this. We are also highly territorial. We can see this in our behaviors in everyday modern life, such as being cut off on the road by another driver, our response is based on 'someone cutting into my lane' attitude. We also see it by the many wars we have committed on each other, primarily tribe to tribe, but also with neighbor to neighbor.

One area that we do have in common with other animals is our sex's influence on killing. It is often the animal's male sex that takes on the role of leader or protector and therefore is the most common killer. But what happened to the male human that allowed him to kill or want to kill outside the most common reasons? Was it the environment? Was it the people who raised him? Or perhaps it was some traumatic event that happened to him when he was young.

Even though all of these are possible contributors to the act of murder if it was just the environment or how someone was raised, why wouldn't murder be even more common? After all, many people have had awful upbringings, or major traumas happen to them at a very young age, yet they live a very normal and non-violent life as an adult.

So, what happened with David Shearing? What was it that made him feel okay with the murder of a family for the reasons of having sex with two minors? I don't think that we will know the answer to this now or ever. What I can add is some of the newer things Shearing described to me.

In the summer of 1982, two girls playing in the old, abandoned prison site in Wells Gray Park, where he was living, caught his attention on his way home from work. He was 23-years old then, and the girls were 13 and 11-years old. It wasn't the case that he heard their laughter while playing, didn't pay much attention, and just went home. He actually stopped, and instead of making himself known to the girls, he hid behind some bushes and watched them.

As they frolicked around the old empty cells, running in and out of each of the buildings, trying to catch each other, playing some tag game, Shearing began to make his plans. "I don't know what happened to me. It's like everything in my mind was gone, and all I could think about was those girls," Shearing admitted.

If something took control of his mind, almost like it wasn't his own, had this happened to him before? "I've had dreams both in the day and at night, but nothing like what happened that day. As much as I didn't like what I was thinking, I couldn't stop it." So much happens in a day around us and far away, but all that matters would be what happened here. There would be changes in many people's lives made that day, and nothing could ever bring the innocence back to us.

How long did Shearing stay and watch the girls?

When did he formulate his plan for what was about to happen? "I'm not sure how long it was, it seemed like it was only five minutes, but I know it was longer, much longer. When I finally got home that night, it was getting dark, and that doesn't happen until about 9 p.m. in August." Shearing cleaned up and went to bed. He had no memory of anything else that night. He felt exhausted, so he fell asleep as soon as he laid down. He never stirred the whole night, and not a thing disturbed his sleep. It would probably be his last night of what he considered peace for the rest of his life.

According to Shearing, the next day was just like every other day. Shearing rose when the sun came up, sometime around 5 a.m., and drank his morning coffee to help wake up. Then he walked to work. The entire workday was as every other day, except for a storm that seemed to be on the horizon. It was still very hot, but clouds had been building throughout the afternoon. The area would have some pretty wicked thunderstorms in summer, loud and flashy, but never lasting more than an hour or two.

When Shearing headed back to his cabin after work, he walked by the old prison. That was the first time he thought about the girls since the night before. "I just wondered if they would be there again, but they weren't. Maybe they had gone home or moved to a different area?" David continued back home to his cabin and made some dinner. It wasn't until later on that evening, somewhere around 7 or 8 p.m., that he thought about the girls again. "I was really curious if they had left for good or not, so I thought I'd go and check things out." He headed out on a search to find the girls and see if they were still camping around the area.

The evening was pretty cloudy, and it made things seem darker than they usually were at 8 p.m. It didn't take long for Shearing to see the flames of the Johnson campfire. He headed toward it until he could hear the voices of people, talking and laughing. He crouched down behind a set of bushes and listened to them for a while and watched when he could. "I just wanted to see if I could spot the same two girls that I had seen before and see if they were there," Shearing said.

"So, you're just wanting to see if they were there, and not gone from the campsite, and nothing more?" I asked.

"Yeah, I had no other intentions at all," he replied.

However, in my research, I had seen several other pieces of information claiming Shearing sat on the hill behind the bushes and fantasized about the girls while masturbating. When I asked about this,

Shearing answered, "No, I would not masturbate. I was unable to get myself up, you know. I have always had a problem with that. I can still think about things, but usually don't get them."

Shearing claimed that after he saw the two girls were still at the campsite, he just went back to his cabin and went to bed. I can't help but wonder what was really running through his mind that night. Did he honestly just go to sleep thinking nothing more of the girls, or did he continue to fantasize about them? After all, the next day was when it all happened. Could he have just woke up and snapped?

The next morning, the third day that Shearing knew about the girl's location started the same as the previous day had. Shearing made coffee, got ready, and walked to work. But on this day, he claimed that after work, he never went back by the campsite where the family was. Instead, he went straight home. Could it be that because he saw the girls were camping with four adults, and two of those men had swayed him from ever thinking he could somehow get the girls? After all, there were four of them and only one of him. The men were both hunters too, so it was more than likely they would have firearms with them. But that night, something happened that changed everything, not just for the Johnson and Bentley families that were camping, but for the whole country. Something that would be talked about for years to come.

Later that night, we know that again, Shearing walked over to the spot where he had watched the family around their campfire a few nights earlier. And like before, he squatted down, hidden behind the shrubs and shadows that ran through the cloudy night. When he first arrived, he spotted the girls right away, as they were laughing and showing off what looked like some fish that they must have caught earlier in the day, like it was a first-time thing. After a little while, Jackie Johnson got the girls settled down and into the tent for the night.

"So, if you never had any thoughts the night before, or all this day, why did you find yourself at the camp again?" I asked. Shearing replied, "I was just fascinated with who they were, and how well they were getting along. Being a family."

Probably only an hour or two later, Shearing walked into their campsite with a gun. So what happened from when he was enjoying watching family time with the Johnsons, to when he actually approached them? We were only minutes away from the start of a brutal carnage of a family. "I was like in a trance. I was drawn to the glow of the campfire. I just wanted to get closer to the girls, and maybe somehow, I would be able to see them again or get them to come with me."

Shearing approached the camp from behind the campfire, somewhere between the tent and camper. It was the perfect spot to keep an eye on all four of the adults, and perhaps sneak into the tent, if not now, maybe after they went to bed in the camper.

From Shearing's perspective, there were three of them standing and one seated around the fire. Suddenly one of the women stood up and appeared to be looking directly at Shearing. "I was scared, and jumped forward, told them not to move as I had a gun. I didn't know what I was going to do next. I really didn't. But she started to scream, and one of the guys started to run for the truck, so I had to shoot."

Shearing shot Bob Johnson in the neck, which made him fall to the ground while clutching his neck in an attempt to try and stop the bleeding. He then ran towards the camper to stop the Grandfather from getting his rifle and shot him in the back of the head. As he walked around the back of the truck, Grandma Bentley was at the camper door, trying to open it. He shot her in the back of the head, and she fell to the ground. Then as he walked back to the center of the camp, he saw Jackie Johnson opening up the tent zipper door. So he crept up behind her and shot her in the back of the head too.

Shearing said he pushed his head in the open tent doorway to check on the girls. "Hey, are you guys alright?" He said, "Both of them were lying on their stomachs and looking up toward the open door. And they looked scared, so I decided to get into the tent with them to calm them down."

What he did when he went into the tent is questionable. Shearing just recounted that there was screaming and yelling and four rifle shots just outside of their tent. The girls were 11 and 13, old enough to know that the sound of shots fires and screams meant something terrible was happening. So, when a gruff looking man, a stranger, carrying a rifle, came into their tent right after their mother, they'd be at the least scared and probably crying frantically.

Shearing initially told the detectives that he shot both girls in the head. He then removed each of the children's bodies and placed them into the trunk of their parent's car. After that, he loaded the four adults in the back seat, covered them with a blanket, and drove the car towards a gully where he burned it to hide all the evidence.

But then we discover that's not what really happened at all. Shearing did shoot the four adults as he said he did, but not the two girls. In Shearing's second confession, he told Eastham that he got into the tent with the girls, told them some bad people were out there, and their parents went to get help. He also said he told the girls that their parents wanted them to stay with him until they got back. Given their ages and what they witnessed, it is unimaginable that the girls didn't know what was going on. They might not have understood why it was happening or what was going to happen to them, but they knew there was something wrong.

Shearing now said that he shot Jackie Johnson while she was opening the tent door, and her body fell in the doorway of the tent, right in front of the girls. Jackie's body held the unzipped tent doors open, and both girls locked eyes with Shearing's as he stood behind their mother's body, still holding the rifle he used to kill her.

It's impossible now to believe that the girls were in any way calm with Shearing. Not after seeing him shoot their mother and hearing all the other screams and shots that night. But I still asked, "And after they had calmed down and began to trust you?" He replied, "I just wanted them to trust me. I wasn't going to hurt them. I wanted to keep them safe is all. All we did was talk, and tell stories about fishing and the old prison that they liked to play in."

So, what did he really do in that tent? "I got the older one to tie up the younger girl's hands. She wasn't too calm and kept yelling for no reason. I wanted her (Janet) to remove her clothes so I could make her feel good. I wasn't hurting her. Just feeling her. The other didn't understand it and kept crying, so I had to put something in her mouth." When asked if he raped them, he replied, "I couldn't get up. I hadn't for a while. I thought maybe I could if I had them with me, but no. Back then, my fantasies were about younger women, who couldn't laugh at me, and they let me try to get things to work, you know?"

According to him, after he finished with his fantasy play in the tent, he told them to get dressed and stay inside the tent until he called them. He wanted to make sure the bad guys were all gone. What he was really doing was placing the four adult bodies into the back seat of the car and covering them with a blanket. He called the girls out and told them to dismantle the tent and place it in the trunk of the car.

They all got into the front seat of the Plymouth, and he drove back to his cabin. Shearing then found a place on the property for the girls to set up the tent. He told them to stay close, because not only were the bad guys out there, but there were wild animals too. While they put the tent together, he drove the car away, and later returned with the truck and camper. "They really trusted me. They believed everything that I told them. We had become friends. I made them sleep in the tent the first night, and if they got cold, they could come to sleep in the camper with me."

I then asked if they had become friends, and they

not only trusted but liked each other, what happened to make him kill them? "Karen was not going to understand. She didn't work with me. I don't think she could figure out what we needed to do. I tried so many times, but she kept fighting me. The thing is I gave her a whole day with me, by myself. Nobody to bother us so that I could show her how she needed to be. It was not just for me, but for her too. I wanted her to be happy and like being with me. I don't know why, but she would not listen or keep stopping to cry. It wasn't sad. It was good."

In my effort to explain to Shearing, I said, "I don't know David. She just couldn't comprehend what sex was at 11. She didn't have that same upbringing or lack of parenting that you had."

With this latest claim, it's hard to tell how the killings really happened with the two girls. He claimed that he first killed Janet, the 13-year-old, then after spending a day with Karen, he killed her.

Next, our discussion went to being released from prison and living on parole in the outside world, and why that would be okay for him. "I have always been impotent, and never really successful in having sex, proper sex. I used to have fantasies where I could use bondage to control anyone that I would want to have sex with. It was always with young girls because it would be easier to control. I wouldn't have to hurt them. Women tend to be stronger and can put up a fight. It wasn't meant to hurt them, the bondage, it was so that I could control them, help them enjoy it. I wasn't going to rape them. I just wanted to touch them, kiss them, smell them. They would like that too. But these fantasies went away. They started when I was 15, and after Janet, they were gone. I don't have them anymore. When I was 15, they started to grow with intensity and brutality over the years. Together with my hatred for the world and how it treated me and my family, I was able to kill the adults. I just wanted to live out my fantasies of bondage and dominance over Janet, the 13-year-old. This also gave me a sense of worth or power over the world that I hated so much. I no longer have desires for young girls, or to do drugs, or have those kinds of fantasies anymore."

Back in Shearing's parole hearing held in 2008, he said that he wanted the Johnsons and Bentleys to know what really happened to the girls, rather than have them believe things that did not happen. Shearing said, "I struck Janet in the stomach and ordered her to remove her clothes. She did, and then she started to cry. I lost the excitement that I had felt. I wasn't able to continue any of the sadistic parts."

Shearing described his feelings about his sexual fantasies. "I was angry at the world because I thought that I didn't fit in and that I was ugly. I became very shy. I think I was angry at the whole world, and it came out against women. I am not a pedophile and have never had fantasies about children." To Shearing, a child was a girl under 15-years old. He thought Janet was older than 13.

As to the shooting of the two girls in the head and why he did that, he responded, "I was thinking about myself. I reasoned that I had already committed the murders. I couldn't let them go because I would be in a lot of trouble. Now, when I think of it, I wish I hadn't."

Shearing admitted that he continued to fantasize about his assaults on Janet and Karen for about the first ten years in prison. Eventually, they started to diminish in intensity and now have disappeared completely. "For a while, I wished I had been able to fulfill the fantasies I had about Janet and Karen so that I would have known what it meant. Or at least I think I would have understood it better." Shearing said that he never learned how to deal with his feelings or emotions properly when he was a child.

When Shearing was first caught, and on trial, he said that it made him feel important for the first time in his life, almost like a celebrity. All the other inmates looked up to him and seemed to admire and respect him. Remember, though, that at the time of the arrest and trial, nothing about the children's sexual assault was known. The other prisoners only knew of him as a killer of six, maybe seven people. If the truth were known to the public at that time, the other inmates would have been trying to kill him.

In a famous, but not so different case, on January 15, 1974, four Otero family members were murdered in Wichita, Kansas. The victims were Joseph Otero, age 38; Julie Otero, age 33; Joseph Otero Jr., age 9; and Josephine Otero, age 11. Their bodies were discovered by the family's eldest child, who was in 10th grade. Dennis Rader, depressed after being laid off, was "trolling" one day when he spotted Julie leaving to take her children to school. He liked the dark hair, skin, and eyes of Latinas. Struck by Julie's beauty and taken with young Josie, he followed them to school. The mother and daughter were his perfect victims. Nearly two months later, fueled by thoughts of bondage, Rader lived out his sexual fantasies through the Otero family. He would later tell police that the basement was "symbolic, like a dungeon." Hanging was a central element of his fantasies. "… So my encore was to just take her down there and hang her. If she had been dead, I would have still hung her, just to hang her." In the basement, a rope was already prepared to hang Josie. To watch her struggle for her life, she was hung so that her toes barely brushed the ground as the noose suspended from a sewer pipe. For "a sexual release," he pulled down her panties. Police found his semen traces near her body. Rader, aka The BTK Killer (Bind, Torture, Kill), was sentenced to 10 life sentences, or 175 years – one for each life he took. He is in the most restrictive prison possible, allowed out for one hour a day, five days a week, to shower and/or exercise.

Today, Shearing claims that he now sees the damage that he has done. "Just knowing that I am responsible for all of that devastating loss causes me to be sick to my stomach. I actually hate being in my own skin so much that I'll find myself scratching my arms hard, sometimes until I bleed. I have wanted to apologize to the families in person for so long now. I have taken away their most valuable things to them. For this loss, I am sincerely sorry. I am so sorry for all of the grief and pain that I have caused."

Shearing said that he wished he could be moved from medium to minimum security and hopefully be allowed someday to have day passes. "My wish is to put what time I have left to some good use. I would be thankful and proud to be able to help support my wife." Continuing, he states, "My crime was caused by a unique sense of circumstances and problems, and those problems have been resolved. My psychologist says I'm ready to begin the process towards release."

FIGHT FROM THE INSIDE | 171

Bowden Institution

I'm sure a lot of you have never been to a prison in Canada and don't know what it's like there, or how the inmates live. Below is a description of what the institute that Shearing has been living in is like and the current problems that the prison has.

Bowden Institution is a medium-security prison operated by Correctional Services Canada. It was built on an "open campus" model. Bowden Institution is separated into Medium and Minimum Federal security sections. The Medium section opened in 1974 and can house 450 adult male inmates. The minimum-security area was built in 1992 and can accommodate 120 inmates living in simulated residential housing units.

In 2012/2013, an additional 96 man receiving unit was constructed inside the medium-security unit, and an additional 5, 10-man housing units were constructed at the minimum-security annex. Currently, the medium-security unit houses two men per cell in the majority of the cells.

The facility is located on Alberta's Queen Elizabeth II Highway, between the small towns of Bowden and Innisfail, Alberta, approximately halfway between Calgary and Edmonton.

The Bowden Institution is the only prison in Alberta that offers a high-intensity sex offender program. The program begins with a six-week primer program and then consists of 117 classroom sessions over about four and a half months.

When I first arrived at the institute, I was reminded of a high school that I once attended back in the seventies. The parking is on the right side of the main building, and when you enter, you are required to sign in a visitor's log. You then go through a metal detector, and all loose items have to be removed from your pocket and placed on a desk, to be searched. The institution officers take anything that they figure to be an issue and place them into a locker. You are not permitted to bring any recording equipment or cameras into the prison.

You are then required to hand in your photo identification (driver's license), and in return, I was given a visitor's card that you have to clip onto your shirt collar so that its visible at all times while you are there. Each visit can only last 20 minutes long, and you are only allowed two visits per week.

When you're on a cell block, there can be 50 to 120 inmates, and there are two officers to observe that area, three officers at most. It really is a relaxed atmosphere as far as prisons go. Throughout the prison, there's a clinical smell that wafts through the hallways, sort of like a hospital.

To give you an idea of who is housed there, in February 2014, former Guantanamo captive, Omar Khadr was transferred to the institution from the Millhaven maximum security facility. At Bowden, Khadr had programs available to him, which helped him apply for parole.

One of the largest problems in Bowden is drug usage by the inmates. Just last year, an estimated $384,000 worth of street drugs was seized there. On March 11, 2019, as a result of the vigilance of staff members, packages containing contraband were seized near the minimum-security unit. The contraband seized included crystal methamphetamine, shatter (THC concentrate), and two cellphones. Drugs are illegal and enter prisons in Canada through an array of means, one being the use of drones, which drop packages into areas accessible by inmates.

In response to the drug issues, this year, the prison has started a prison needle exchange program – a program that allows prisoners to possess needles so that they can take drugs in their cell whenever they want. The problem is once a needle goes onto that living unit, it is open for everybody to share and use, and becomes difficult to keep track of.

The next question you might think of might be, 'With such light security in Bowden prison, how about escapes?' Here, there's a little better news. As far as I could find out, there has only been one escape in the last five years from Bowden, but there was a guard involved in helping with that escape. Peter Edgar, a former production supervisor with Correctional Service Canada, pleaded guilty in Red Deer provincial court to permitting or assisting escape. Edgar, 61, at the time, was working on a program that provides incarcerated offenders with job-skills training. He was charged following the 2015 escape of Sylvain Martin from Bowden Institution. Following his arrest, Martin told police that while he was an inmate, he developed a relationship with Edgar, who provided Martin with a phone and $5,000 prior to his escape. Martin was serving a 10-year sentence for fraud when he fled from the prison's minimum-security wing. He made his way to Calgary and then on to Quebec, where he was taken into custody.

| Bowden Institution

---

1. R. Douglas Fields, Why We Snap, p. 286, 2016

THERE'S NO PLACE FOR US

Heather was working and living in Prince Albert, Saskatchewan, when she first contacted David Shearing. She first sent him a letter through one of the many websites that offer the ability to become pen-pals with an inmate. She said that she felt connected to David from the very first word that he wrote to her.

On October 22, 2008, they were married in a small jailhouse ceremony, attended by only themselves and two witnesses required by law. They get two 72-hour family visits every month, where they live just like a family in the outside world in a small housing unit on the penitentiary grounds. The unit looks like a small apartment-style house, with a real bed, real bathroom, and kitchen. From the inside, there is nothing that would give away the fact that it is located in a field surrounded by guards with weapons and a wired fence.

They have a television and a sofa where they can snuggle and watch most shows that you and I can-all while having homemade popcorn or any delight she can bring into the house to enjoy together. They can retire to their bedroom and enjoy time in each other's arms all night. Their mornings can include quiet coffee time, reading, and maybe a game of cards. "I know my husband, and I've watched him cry like you'd never believe. Nobody wishes the past could be changed more than him." Heather claims.

She doesn't expect anybody to feel sorry for David or believe his anguish over the grisly murders of the Johnson and Bentley families. "I understand why people have feelings of revulsion or dismay once they discover that I am married to him and have been for over 27 years now. People will ask me, 'How the hell did you marry him?' If I didn't really love him, or believe in him, I couldn't have stayed married to him this long, could I?"

After a quick sigh and short pause, she continued, "I can say that he's not the same human being as he was back then." With disdain, she pretends to be someone responding to her statement, 'Talk about naïve, are you stupid?' "I don't blame people if they haven't forgiven him, but I have forgiven him, as my husband and as a human being. I think every human being under the laws of God deserves a second chance."

The room was now silent. I'm not sure, but I think Heather was waiting for some emotional response from me, but I remained stone-faced, as I usually do. I'm not oblivious to the frustration she feels in others, or her anguish for this to all be over. But being on the autism spectrum, I seem to be able to compartmentalize things. When people speak about me, sometimes they will say that I'm cold or have no feelings, but that's simply not true. It comes as a great advantage to me while researching and in live interviews that I can stick to the facts and keep things clear in my mind.

Heather continues, "I doubt that David will be let go anytime soon, because no one believes that he has paid his debt, except for me. I pray that it will happen every night, but no, I just don't think so. I think it'll be a long time before he is free."

When is a debt paid for a crime like this? Can it ever be settled? Why is it she thinks Shearing's debt can be paid by serving time in prison? I got the feeling that God plays a significant part in her life. So much so that her life is not only dedicated to her religion, but her life revolves around it. That said, even if it were true that Shearing has found God, and in her eyes been forgiven by that same God, does that mean he should be free to live a full life with the time he has left? I'm still at a point in my life where I believe we should be judged only by the things we do, our actions, and not by what are beliefs are.

"Someone told me he'd gone ten years without contact from anybody. I think that everyone deserves some contact with the outside world, no matter what they've done, that's just my forgiving nature."

Perhaps the outside world doesn't want to be in contact with him. I don't have any children of my own, but I can only imagine those who do would not want Shearing out free, living as their neighbor.

Trying to change the subject, she told me that if he were to be released, it would be the first time that they could live a life as a loving couple without being watched or behind locks for the first time. "But how are the surviving family members supposed to live with that?" I asked.

"I love this man from the bottom of my heart. It didn't start out like that, but I do. He's very, very, very nice and a good man and nobody's sorry like him. He prays every single day, and it's the hardest part for him. He does this all while knowing that freedom may never come for him." I'm guessing from that kind of an answer, it's all about Shearing feeling bad or sorry for what he's done to those families, and when we are sorry for the bad things that we do, we are forgiven and should be free to live our lives.

Heather has had her share of bad things happen to her because of her marriage to Shearing. She lost her job as a senior's center manager in Prince Albert, Saskatchewan, and as an elk's club bar manager. She has sued for wrongful dismissal and made some progress, but now remains in hiding from the public regarding her current job and residence. Eventually, Heather won a settlement of about $2,000 for the wrongful termination of her job.

So, how does she reconcile with what Shearing did to those two children? "I can't. I don't know what happened back then. It was something more than a bad day. We have to put our trust in God. Whatever it was that caused him to do those things are now gone. I know he has a good soul and that he is not that person anymore."

MARRIAGE WITH AN INMATE

Like Heather, why do so many people marry inmates? Why would a 26-year-old woman marry an 80-year-old maniac Charles Manson? Yes, a few devote themselves to the madmen and sociopaths like Manson. Many others find matches of convenience or even love. Do you ever wonder how or why a woman marries a serial killer that's been sentenced to life in prison? Why is it that every time a man gains infamy for unimaginably brutal crimes of rape, murder, and torture, women are knocking down his prison cell trying to put a ring on his finger? It seems the more heinous the crime, the more likely an inmate is to receive fan mail from women. Who would seek out connection, particularly a love connection, with a serial killer?

If you watched *Making a Murderer*, you were probably fascinated by the part where Steven Avery gained a new love interest while incarcerated. You may also remember the prison worker in 2013 who helped two inmates escape from a New York prison because of her claim that they were in a romantic relationship. Other notorious prison marriages or committed relationships include serial killers John Wayne Gacy, Ted Bundy, The Hillside Strangler, and the Menendez brothers. Reportedly, the Oklahoma City bomber, Timothy McVeigh, and killer Scott Peterson, imprisoned for killing his wife and unborn child, receive countless letters from would-be suitors.

There are a growing number of programs that support letter-writing with inmates. The very day Scott Peterson entered San Quentin for murdering his wife and son, he received three dozen phone calls from female admirers and a marriage proposal from an 18-year-old girl.

As for the reasons why? Some women become fixated with these killers because of their popularity with the media. Many of these women cannot find love, so they pretend this is love. And some women don't want to have to deal with a guy every day. There's an increasing number of women who want to date, have sex with or marry death row prisoners. Some women find that sexy.

"**Hybristophilia**" is now a recognized mental condition where someone—most always a woman—has intense sexual arousal from a man who's committed a notorious crime, or experiences strong sexual desire for a man known for crimes society considers repulsive. The "philia" comes from the Greek word meaning "love for," while "hybristo" is derived from the Greek verb meaning "to commit an outrage against someone." It is also known as "Bonnie & Clyde Syndrome," and the condition can manifest in passive or aggressive forms.

Passive hybristophiliacs avoid crime and usually cultivate a safe relationship while their lover boy is tucked away behind bars. They tend to delude themselves into thinking that their Death Row fiancé is entirely innocent, and even if they don't, they're confident he'd never harm them. Their attraction is more of the nurturing type in that they feel empathy for the lonely and wrongly accused little boy trapped behind bars.

Aggressive hybristophiliacs are fully aware that they get wetter than a floor mop at the idea of a violent, murderous thug. They often are complicit in their lovers' crimes and will even help them hide bodies or destroy evidence.

Hybristophilia is recognized as a potentially lethal disorder. The book *Dream Lovers: Women Who Marry Men Behind Bars* details the sad case of two Australian women named Avril and Rose, who abandoned their long-term marriages because they were "boring." They both fell in love with two convicts—a thief and a man who'd killed his previous wife. A week after being released, Avril's lover (the thief) beat her to death with a hammer. Rose's boyfriend, whom she proclaimed, "I have no fear," was sent back to prison after trying to cut off her ear and haul out her teeth with pliers.

Psychologists offer an array of speculations for what causes the disorder. A running theme is that in a world where men's roles and values are diminishing, the serial killer triggers ancient instincts and represents a sort of heroically Promethean-like being, the alpha caveman whose bravery and ruthlessness demonstrates he'd be able to protect a woman and her offspring. Although "nice guys" may seem desirable in a high-tech world, they wouldn't provide much protection when there's a saber-tooth tiger at the door.

Women find strength and empowerment when they feel as if they are "rescuing" their partners. Those who are more likely to feel connected and fall in love with someone who is being punished for a crime are typically people who have a history of abuse or low self-esteem, so their overall self-concept is lower. Often, if they have suffered abuse, some women feel safer in relationships where their partner physically can't touch them. People who crave constant stimulation or excitement may find it quite attractive to land the "bad boy." This type of relationship provides a continuous thrill and the ability to create one's own story in many ways rather than having to truly settle into an honest emotional connection with someone.

Prisons are economic entities where items in low supply and high demand are worth more. Cigarettes and stamps, in lieu of currency, keep the market liquid. Inmates with money to shop is a kind of status assertion. They purchase the best radios, finest sneakers, and snazziest glasses. But there are limits to what a prisoner may possess, so the item most rare - a wife or girlfriend - is also the most valued. Sometimes this leads to marital transactions, a classic jailhouse hustle. It is somewhere between slavery and matchmaking.

A spouse who "looks out" on the outside, keeping the inmate's interest in mind, is a valued commodity. In prison, the word "woman" was rare, "female" was polite, and "bitch" was commonplace. There is even a slang term for a wife kept while incarcerated, a "buck-35," which means a woman sending a hundred dollars a month and 35 pounds of food. Many unmarried convicts settle for homosexual admirers with credit cards on the outside.

Pen pals are encouraged to keep it platonic or to inspire the inmate's spiritual development. Of course, this compassion sometimes is misconstrued for or truly leads to amorous love. Most inmates want companionship just like everyone else, and the mission of the 12 prison dating sites below is to help them build those human connections and reintegrate with society. Inmates can find a caring pen pal, a fun date, or even a life-long relationship on these welcoming sites. It's a freeing experience that could lead to something truly remarkable:

- Meet an Inmate
- Canadian Inmates Connect Inc.
- Dating Prisoners
- Inmate Mingle
- Inmate Classified
- Love A Prisoner
- Inmate Passions

- Match.com
- Friends Beyond the Wall
- Prison Inmates
- Write A Prisoner
- Women Behind Bars

Many individuals in the world are in a healthy and mutually beneficial relationship, of which a major part involves face to face interaction and touch. These people might be baffled as to who would be drawn to someone they will rarely (or never) see in person and not ever have moments that couples out in the world enjoy.

According to recent statistics, more than 2.3 million Americans are incarcerated in correctional facilities, including local jails, state prisons, or federal prisons. Dr. Joan Harvey, a psychologist at Newcastle University, explains, "Many people who visit prisoners believe they are there because life has not been kind to them, that it might not be entirely their fault. They may be the do-gooder type who's been touched by the image of the lonely 'victim' in his prison cell. But if they really wanted to help, it would be best to pick someone who could turn themselves around with a bit of support and self-esteem. With a serial killer, you aren't going to do any good. The chances of them turning themselves around are next to nil.

Forensic psychologist, Katherine Ramsland, said,

"Some believe they can change a man as cruel and powerful as a serial killer. Others 'see' the little boy that the killer once was and seek to nurture him. A few hoped to share in the media spotlight or get a book or movie deal."

In 1995, 544 inmates were married in New York State prisons, which house 68,000 inmates, the third-largest population in the country, after California and Texas. Of those married, 42% of the prisoners have Grade 12 or less, while 64% of their spouses have post-secondary school.

An examination of the characteristics of the inmates and their spouses in this study found that

- The majority (56%) of the inmates were serving life sentences,
- The majority of inmates and spouses reported completing secondary school,
- One-third of the spouses were currently unemployed, and
- One-third of spouses had an income below $12,000.

The majority of couples (78%) had children from previous relationships, and 42% had at least one child under 19. Of 36 marriages in prison in 1995, 18 (or 50%) met during incarceration and married in prison. 38% of the mothers had two or more children over

18, and 32% had two or more children under 18. Of all the prisoners that marry, 56% are serving life sentences.

When it comes to wearing jewelry, although prisoners are allowed to have an extremely limited range of personal jewelry (including plain wedding rings), big, chunky bling is banned. Specific examples are rings with gemstones or heavy patterns and medallions on heavy chains (other than small religious symbols, such as crucifixes.)

In Canada, all inmates, except those on disciplinary restrictions or at risk for family violence, are permitted "private family visits" of up to 72 hours duration once every two months.

The stays, which remain a part of the Canadian correctional system, are linked to a long-standing program aimed at increasing the inmate's chances of successfully reintegrating into society after their release. Some experts say Canada's private family visit program, which began in 1980 as a pilot project, plays an important role in rehabilitating offenders. It also provides corrections officers with a useful tool for encouraging good behavior from inmates.

The program has received recent attention after a media report that Kelly Ellard, a notorious killer in British Columbia, is eight-months pregnant following a conjugal visit from her boyfriend. Lisa Kerr, a law professor at Queen's University in Kingston, Ont., said the program recognizes that the majority of federal inmates will be released and that it is in society's best interest to make that process as successful as possible.

"Close personal relationships are part of what makes people have hope about their future and gives them a reason to invest in their correctional programming and move toward a release plan," she said.

Canada's longtime correctional investigator, Howard Sapers, said conjugal visits have been around for as long as he can remember. He cited research showing inmates who are allowed to maintain close family bonds have a lower likelihood of reoffending.

Jennifer Lutz thought the man she wed behind bars — the same man accused of stabbing her 28 times in a prison yard during a visit to his British Columbia jail for a Christmas social-was her soul mate. The 31-year-old first met Earl Bernard Nantais while visiting a friend in jail more than a decade earlier. Several years later, she got in touch with him through the prison system, and the pair corresponded for several months before setting their wedding date at the B.C. prison last August. "I believed he was my soul mate for years and years," said the mother of three from her home in Chilliwack. "I truly believe it was a soul-mate connection." She said their jailhouse wedding ceremony "was just beautiful." But four months later, Mr. Nantais was arrested and charged with attempted murder, accused of stabbing Ms. Lutz with a makeshift knife as her three sons watched during a Christmas visit to the Kent Institution.

Heather's forgiveness of Shearing for the crimes he committed is quite common among women with boyfriends or husbands that are in prison doing time for violent crimes. So how do they meet? In the U.S. and Canada, the majority of inmates do have access to the internet. So, the online pen-pal sites and apps make the correspondence and eventual relationship possible. The meeting website will list all the prisoners that want to be involved in finding someone. Each inmate can be searched out by age, zodiac sign, ethnicity, and their sentences.

Corrections Canada encourages convicts to form a romantic relationship with people on the outside. The thought behind that is for when the prisoners are released. If they are in a stable, romantic relationship, they have a far better chance of not reoffending. A Simon Fraser University professor says, "95% of murderers in Canada won't return to jail after they're released. They may go back for violating terms of their patrol, but to be convicted of a violent offense after release from a homicide conviction is extremely rare."

According to Sheila Isenberg, author of the book *Women Who Love Men Who Kill,* the real desire for a woman to want a relationship with a violent inmate is the desire to be a vicarious celebrity. "Because Shearing's case was so widely reported and sensational, his wife would fall into the category of women who get involved with serial or mass murderers, or sensational killers, rather than your garden variety murderers. Like someone who's committed one crime and doesn't have a high profile or in the media."

I commented that these days this desire would be even greater because of how big social media has come on over recent years. "Exactly." Isenberg confirmed. "If you're dating someone notorious, you'll put it on your Facebook, Twitter, Instagram, or any other app that you have available." I asked does that really do something good for a person. "Remember, we live in a country that worships violence." Isenberg says. "Violence plays an enormous role in television and films in America and Canada. Because of that, we end up loving the guy who does the shooting, whether he's a good guy or not. We think of them as sexy or a manly man."

Another side to becoming a pen-pal to a prisoner I never considered before researching this book is the physical danger. According to Katherine Ramsland, Ph.D., many inmates sell their pen-pal addresses to other inmates close to being released from prison. "That guy will go to the woman's house and try and get money or something else from them. There are even inmates that are able to manipulate their pen-pal into quitting their jobs, selling their house and anything else that they have, and get them to move real close to the prison, so that they can visit and be close to them. These are often men that have made some tragic mistakes but don't represent any risk in a relationship."

17

MAN ON THE PROWL

After Parole Denied 2012

Bob Johnson's brother, Art, was unsure if he would attend the first parole hearing for David Shearing. "I hope he stays in prison for good! What he did was just cold-blooded murder. Why should he ever get out?" Art Johnson had just turned 76 at the time of the parole hearing, and his health was poor, "I just don't know if I want to go through all this again. I'm not sure that I can handle the stress. He killed three generations of our family; our loss was unbelievable. Bob was my only brother; I'm always seeing things that remind me of him and his family."

Almost 10,000 people from West Kelowna signed a petition supporting that Shearing be denied parole and kept in prison indefinitely. "Their murders were a very emotional event for West Kelowna. The town was a lot smaller back then. And pretty much everyone knew each other," Dorene Lander explained. "It emerged after the Shearing trial that he killed the adults immediately but kept the kids alive for a few days and sexually tortured them." Lander was one of the people that headed up the petition in West Kelowna.

PAROLE HEARING OCTOBER 22, 2008

On Wednesday, October 22, 2008, more than 25 years had passed since he was first convicted and sent to prison. During this time, he decided to change his name to his mother's maiden name, Ennis. So, now he was called David William Ennis by the court reporter. This hearing was his first parole hearing since his conviction of the six murders.

David Shearing was sitting at a table in the prison chapel with his back facing the room. He was ordered by the board not to turn around and face any of the Johnson family members or their supporters. Wearing a red shirt and dark blue jeans that were nicely cleaned and pressed, he no longer had the rugged stocky look he had when he was first arrested.

Behind him, about 2 meters would be all the remaining family, friends, and people who had any personal connection to the victims. This hearing was the first time any of them had seen him since the original trial years ago.

During the hearing, which would last about five hours, the board allowed six victim-impact statements from six people and a statement from Shearing himself and his wife. But the majority of the hearing was the three-panel board members asking Shearing questions. They explored explicit details of his crimes, sexual fantasies, background before prison, prison behavior, and what he had done to rehabilitate himself. This hearing was not a court proceeding, so this was allowed.

They asked him why he should be released as the last question of the hearing where he responded to them. "I endured violent sexual fantasies from the time I was 15 years old. Those fantasies were so strong that it drove me to shoot George and Edith Bentley, their daughter Jackie, and her husband Bob

Johnson while they were camped near my home in Clearwater. I got the adults out of the way so that I could direct my fantasies out on Janet. I had spotted the family camping on a night before, and her blonde hair caught my eye."

Shearing went on to tell the board that he undressed and molested Janet, but never raped her. This admission was the first time any of the victim's families and friends heard the details of the sexual assault on the two girls from Shearing himself.

Shearing then read a ten-minute apology to the family and friends that were present at the hearing. "My crime was an enormous, brutal, and inexcusable tragedy resulting in tremendous loss to the community that I can never make up for. I am deeply ashamed for killing the B.C. family and only want a new beginning." The apology drew sighs from the audience.

"There is no remorse. He's not sorry! I think he was well-rehearsed," said Shelley Boden, the daughter of Bob Johnson's twin sister, Elaine Woods.

The board left the room to deliberate and decide his fate. During that time, Shearing and his wife stayed seated and chatted quietly. But they were even caught laughing a few times.

When the board returned with their verdict, everyone in the audience went silent. Dave Scott, who was heading up this board, stood and read out their decision. "Mr. Ennis, the board's decision is to deny you day or full parole." Shearing showed no reaction as he sat holding his wife's hand as they read the verdict. There was a large sigh of relief throughout the audience. "There will never be any forgiveness," said Michelle Botelho, who attended the hearing with her sisters, the daughters of Jackie's brother Brian Bentley. "I was impressed by the parole board. I don't believe they believed anything he said."

MURDERER ALLOWED OUT ON ESCORTED PASS

Three weeks after Shearing was denied parole by the National Parole board on October 22, 2008, he was granted a four-hour escorted day pass. Corrections Canada notified Shelley Boden that he would be allowed out of prison for about 4 hours on Wednesday, November 12, 2008. Boden is a registered victim and gets notification of Shearing's movements but was shocked to get this call. A few weeks ago, he was denied parole due to the risk he posed on society for future violent offending.

Jeff Campbell of Corrections Canada said that any details on a prisoner's escorted passes fall under the privacy act, and only registered victims are notified. They are typically given the reason for the pass, which often includes medical treatment, court appearance, or mandatory community service. But there are two other possibilities for a day pass that raise concern among the Johnson and Bentley families. Those are the passes given for personal or family contact, listed under the criminal rehabilitation or compassion act. Basically, it allows convicted murderers such as Shearing to visit family members for reasons of compassion with the hope that it might help him to rehabilitate when he's released in the future.

Shearing has also become eligible for unescorted temporary absences. This reward happens once a convict reaches his minimum sentence to be served before he can apply for parole. Shearing met his 25-year minimum back in 2005. So, this makes him eligible to apply for an unescorted day pass now. What's even more disturbing is that he doesn't have to go through the parole board to get them. He can get these passes from the head of the prison institute where he is being held. The institute can give each inmate up to 15 unescorted day passes per year.

This situation eerily reminds me of a case I wrote about several years ago in *Blood Thirst*. The book was about a serial murderer named Wayne Boden, who was convicted of killing five women by drinking their blood from either their necks or breasts while trying to have sex with them. After he was in prison for many years, like Shearing, he was a good prisoner, meaning he never got into any fights or caused trouble. Eventually, this led to him getting escorted day passes in Montreal, just as Shearing did in Red Deer. On Boden's second day-pass, he eluded his guards and ran. He rented a hotel room with an American Express credit card he applied for and received while he was in prison. With that card, he managed to survive out in public for quite a while before getting caught. When he finally did get caught, he was already dating a woman. Can you imagine how she feels now, knowing that she was dating the vampire killer? During Boden's escape, the public was dangerously unaware of what was going on. Could this also be the case if Shearing is out on a day pass, and he, too, gets away from the escorts? To make things even more perilous in Shearing's case, he can also apply for unescorted day passes, which means with no guards.

DAY PASS DENIED NOVEMBER 12, 2008

"It's a great relief to know that I will know why he is getting to leave." Shelley Boden said with great pleasure. "It's a lot of stress on our family." Boden was contacted by Corrections Canada officials and told that Shearing's planned escorted release had been canceled due to treacherous road conditions around the Bowden Institute, which is located near Red Deer,

Alberta. His pass was approved for medical treatment, but the details were not allowed to be disclosed to anybody. Boden asked them if they knew when Shearing's pass would be reissued, and they weren't able to give her an answer.

During these escorted passes, the prisoners are shackled and always accompanied by a minimum of three guards. "I wanted to put the news out there so that the people of Red Deer know that there is going to be a mass killer in their town, and on their streets." Boden asserted, "It's a pretty scary thing that a killer is going to be out and on your streets for four hours. If he were coming my way, I would want to know."

Jeff Campbell of Corrections Canada said that while inmates have access to health care in prisons, an escorted pass could be granted if they have a medical problem that can't be dealt with inside the institute. Under the new policy in 2008, victims of high-profile murder cases and their families will not have to go through the motions of making an official request. They will now be contacted directly from Corrections Canada.

PAROLE HEARING SEPTEMBER 11, 2012

Shearing's second parole hearing occurred on Tuesday, September 11, 2012.

"I continue to be shamed, thoughtful, and aware

of the devastation I have caused," Shearing told the parole board. "My actions will always cause me to feel an overwhelming sense of shame and a lifetime of pain and regret. I am and always will be deeply sorry for the loss I caused them."

The board denied Shearing's parole, and in a statement, said, "It's quite hard to imagine any crimes more serious or more reprehensible than the ones you committed. There still is present a large number of risk concerns."

Shelley Boden, Bob Johnson's niece, after the hearing, said," He said he was sorry for the first time ever. I never heard that before. It took him 30 years to actually feel how sorry you are!"

| Shelley Boden and Kelly Nielsen

We now know that Shearing killed six people in the Johnson and Bentley families for the reason of having sex with their two young girls. Shearing and his supporters, including his wife Heather, suggest that he is better now and no longer has the same fantasies of molesting young girls as he once did.

Sergeant Ron German of the RCMP brought a significant point to my attention that is often overlooked. The night German stopped Shearing and his two buddies in Tumbler Ridge, Shearing didn't think twice about letting German walk to his death as he approached their vehicle. He knew one of his passengers had a loaded rifle and was going to shoot him if he approached the driver's door. Shearing was willing to let German be killed to avoid being caught with the stolen tools in the back of his pick-up. Two days later, when the two officers chased Shearing and his buddy through the bushes and detained them, Shearing, once again, let German walk into his cabin knowing that his buddy, Wyman, was waiting with a loaded 303 rifle. So, twice Shearing was willing to let someone be murdered, and neither of these times had anything to do with gaining access to young girls to have sex.

Even if you believed that Shearing was cured of having fantasies about sex with young girls, what does that behavior say about murder? He proved that he would rather let someone else be killed to save himself from minor arrests for theft in both of those cases. It also exposed the value he has for other people's lives.

It's also important to mention that in Canada if a convicted murderer is sentenced to "life imprisonment," it does not mean actual "life" like it does in some other countries. While an offender will live the remainder of their life under conditions imposed by the criminal justice system, they most likely will not spend the rest of their life in prison. Many will only have to spend a mere seven years behind bars. Their freedoms and mobility, however, will be limited for the rest of their lives. They may be banned from living in certain places or areas, or from communicating with specific people. If they violate the terms of their parole, it can be retracted, forcing them to go back to prison. The average time that those convicted of second-degree murder actually serve in prison is 19.6 years.

There are currently 2,984 murderers in prison in Canada. Statistics show that 22.5% of those serving time for first-degree murder are in minimum-security institutions, as is 30% of inmates convicted of second-degree murder. Combined, 27.5% of violent murderers are in minimum-security prisons.

Worst still, even if an offender is denied parole, they will still likely be released after serving two-thirds of their sentence.

Statistics also show that over 30 murderers in

Canada went on to kill again after being freed from prison between 2000/1 and 2010/11. These figures released by the Home Office show 29 people with homicide convictions went on to commit murder, and six went on to commit manslaughter after being released.

ONCE A PEDOPHILE, ALWAYS A PEDOPHILE?

Shearing now claims to be over his fantasies of performing sexual bondage on underage girls. Does this mean he is "cured"? Is there such a thing as being cured of being a pedophile? This book wouldn't be complete if I didn't look into the latest findings pertaining to pedophiles, what the current treatments are, and if anybody has ever been cured.

FROM THE U.K.'S NHS PORTMAN CLINIC

This 63-year-old's wife left him after his arrest three years ago, his three adult children disowned him, and his siblings became "secondary victims" to the shame of one of society's most reviled crimes. That was all before he was sentenced to a 90-day jail term. But then the former civil servant sought help from the Royal Ottawa Hospital's Sexual Behaviors Clinic, whose unconventional approach to pedophilia has made it an international stand out.

The results seem striking. Following a year or so of therapy that included a steady diet of adult pornography, he says his sexual interests have settled exclusively on age-appropriate women, and young people no longer arouse him. "It frees me, it frees me completely," said the patient about his transformation, asking that his name not be published. "I have nothing to keep inside anymore. I have nothing to hide. It's like a weight that's been lifted."

Indeed, the psychiatric hospital claims not only to make pedophiles less of a risk to society but to essentially cure them — help them shed for good their sexual attraction to pre-pubescent boys and girls.

"I was cured of my pedophilia by the NHS Portman Clinic. I have told the story of my cure several times over the past decade. Briefly, my sexual orientation was wholly pedophiliac. I never offended either directly or indirectly, but I was attracted to pre-adolescent boys of 'choirboy age.' At 21, I sought help from the Portman and was treated

there with psychoanalytic psychotherapy. After three years, I was wholly cured and have been heterosexual ever since. I am now in a committed relationship with several step-grandchildren.

I recently collaborated with a woman who had been on the pedophile spectrum, though the child sexual abuse she suffered was much greater than mine. She successfully resisted the urge to abuse, found a therapist, and rid herself of her pedophiliac urges. She now lives well and happily.

I have been silent on this issue for most of the 42 years since my cure. I am not alone in that silence. There is no cohort of cured and ethical pedophiles advocating for universal treatments for sufferers and an end to their demonization. Not only that, the published accounts of psychoanalytic work with pedophiles are few. Those accounts often refer to private, in-depth psychoanalytic work (multiple sessions per week over long years) with offending pedophiles, and the NHS does not offer such services."

FROM THE U.S.

One psychiatrist, Paul Fedoroff, from the University of Ottawa, takes a different stance than most. He recently published a paper titled: "Can people with pedophilia change? Yes, they can!"

Fedoroff's perspective is that pedophilia is not a sexual orientation; instead, he characterizes it as a "sexual interest" or something that a person happens to want to do sexually. Sexual interest, he says, is something that we acquire from learning, experience, and observation. As such, it is "changeable throughout life."

Fedoroff says that "there is no evidence to suggest that sexual interest is different in terms of changeability compared to (for example) interest in vegetarianism, or kale or oysters." In other words, in his view, just as you can continually learn new food preferences, you can learn new sexual preferences. To be clear, though, he is not arguing that you can change your sexual orientation.

So convinced of this idea is Fedoroff that he recently said in a book: *"Now I routinely tell new patients [with pedophilia] that their prognosis is excellent and that they can expect to have no evidence of disease in less than a year."*

But what evidence is there that pedophiles can

indeed change? So far, there's only one published study offering any support for this idea. The study, on which Fedoroff was an author, involved looking at 43 men who underwent genital arousal testing on two different occasions. At each testing session, participants listened to spoken erotic scenarios depicting children or adults. At the same time, erectile changes were recorded with a penile plethysmograph, which is a ring that goes around the penis and measures changes in blood flow.

During the initial testing period, all the men showed a pedophilic arousal pattern, meaning the stories of children turned them on. However, in a future test, about half of these men (49 percent) showed a change in their arousal pattern. Their arousal to children went down while their arousal to adults went up. We can't say why, however, because this wasn't a treatment study. Participants were selected solely on the basis of having taken the test twice, regardless of whether they underwent treatment.

That boast has garnered widespread attention and accolades for the clinic headed by psychiatrist Dr. Paul Fedoroff. The clinic won a gold achievement award in 2015 from the American Psychiatric Association, which praised the unit for its innovative approach and apparent success.

But many experts remain highly skeptical, saying

scientific evidence indicates pedophilia is, in fact, unchangeable, as hard-wired for men as being heterosexual or gay. They argue that Fedoroff's one major study to back up his hypothesis is deeply flawed and worry about the impact of sending pedophiles off into the world convinced their cursed predilection had been defeated.

LATEST TREATMENTS

Pedophilia, the sexual attraction to children who have not yet reached puberty, remains a vexing challenge for clinicians and public officials. Classified as a paraphilia, abnormal sexual behavior, researchers have found no effective treatment. Like other sexual orientations, pedophilia is unlikely to change. Therefore, the goal of treatment is to prevent someone from acting on pedophile urges — either by decreasing sexual arousal around children or increasing the ability to manage that arousal. But neither is as effective for reducing harm as preventing access to children or providing close supervision.

A consensus now exists that pedophilia is a distinct sexual orientation, not something that develops in a homosexual or heterosexual. Some people with pedophilic urges are also attracted to adults and may act only on the latter urges. Because people with pedophilic urges tend to be attracted to children of a particular gender, they can be described as heterosexual, homosexual, or bisexual pedophiles. Roughly 9% to 40% of pedophiles are homosexual in their orientation toward children — but that is not the same as saying they are homosexual. Homosexual adults are no more likely than heterosexuals to abuse children.

Several reports have concluded that most people with pedophilic tendencies eventually act on their sexual urges somehow. Typically, this involves exposing themselves to children, watching naked children, masturbating in front of children, or touching children's genitals. Oral, anal, or vaginal penetration is less common.

Cognitive-Behavioral Therapy

Most psychotherapies used to treat pedophilia incorporate the principles and techniques of cognitive-behavioral therapy. The focus of treatment is to enable the patient to recognize and overcome rationalizations about his behavior. It can also involve empathy training and techniques for sexual impulse control.

The most common type of cognitive-behavioral therapy used with offenders (relapse prevention) is similar to addiction treatment. Relapse prevention is intended to help anticipate situations that increase the risk of sexually abusing or assaulting a child, and find ways to avoid or respond to them. Reviews that have included uncontrolled and nonrandomized studies concluded that relapse prevention programs reduced recidivism. Only one randomized controlled trial has evaluated how effective a relapse prevention program was, however, and it included sex offenders who had assaulted adults and those who hurt children. After an average of eight years, there was no significant difference in recidivism between sex offenders who underwent relapse prevention therapy and controls who did not undergo treatment.

Aversive Conditioning

Another popular behavioral treatment for pedophilia was aversive conditioning. This type attempted to associate a pedophilic fantasy or desire with an unpleasant sensation such as nausea, an electric shock, or a bad smell. Although a review concluded that aversive conditioning might help someone's ability to control sexual attraction to children in the short term, there was no evidence that this approach was effective over time.

Drug Treatments

There are drugs that suppress the production of the male hormone testosterone. These can be used to reduce the frequency or intensity of sexual desire. Although physical castration is another option, testosterone suppression offers advantages such as the need for follow-up visits (which aids in monitoring behavior). It may take three to 10 months for testosterone suppression to reduce sexual desire.

19

PAROLE FOR KILLERS IN CANADA

One of the most common things that I hear from people who talk to me about crime and murder cases in Canada and the United States is that most criminals and killers get caught, tried, and convicted, but never really get punished enough. In some cases, the people saying this to me are usually the families or friends of the victims, and in those cases, nothing short of death would be punishment enough. Nevertheless, society's general perception is that too many are not punished appropriately for their crimes.

How many times have you heard things like, "Can you believe it, that lady killed her three kids, and only got five years!" or something like, "Yeah, that guy had been away for rape and murder before but was let out after seven years, and he's done it again! So much for justice!"

The keyword here is justice. What does that mean to you when you hear it? What exactly is justice anyway? When I was a young kid, I heard that word a lot from adults, or the 1970s crime shows I used to watch like *Starsky & Hutch* or *Barretta. (Robert Blake sure had his own first-hand experience with the real justice system when he was arrested for murdering his then-wife)*

With the recent surge in the popularity of true crime shows and news broadcasted on every streaming service, television network, radio, and now even podcasts, you would think most of us would know a lot more about our justice system. But we honestly don't. This easy access to crime shows and crime news might be a contributing factor to people's frustration over the justice system since the result often turns out so differently from what they expect.

So, is the justice system as easy on convicted murderers as we think it is? I figured that since it was such an important part of this case and an issue for many in society, I would look at what the laws are in Canada regarding convicted killers and parole. I will also look at who is on parole boards, their job description, and how we interact with them as a society.

Regarding sentences in cases like the one written about in this book, I cannot say whether they are right or wrong. That's something that the country has to come together on and decide. But what I can offer is an opinion. And as far as I'm concerned, after encountering David Shearing from this case, I feel quite comfortable saying that criminals like him should never be allowed back into general society. They have lost that right because of the violent acts they have committed on innocent families without mercy.

We are not equipped to heal or cure such violent people as Shearing, and that alone should be enough to keep them separate from the rest of society. It's not just about rehabilitation, as our prisons are primarily just a place to house these criminals. Even if all the mental treatments that could cure them were possible, most inmates wouldn't get them. Many of these convicted killers and rapists deny the criminal acts they have committed to others. Therefore, they see no need to get any treatment, as in their minds, they've done nothing wrong.

So, let's take a look at the Shearing murder case to understand why he is up for release on parole, who and what the parole is, what they are trying to do with the criminal, and how the victim's family is involved.

WHAT DOES A LIFE SENTENCE IN CANADA MEAN?

In 1976, the Federal government revoked the death penalty and introduced mandatory terms of life imprisonment for individuals convicted of first and second-degree murder. First-degree and two categories of second-degree murder have a minimum parole ineligibility period of 10 years, to a maximum of 25 years.

A concurrent sentence means multiple sentences will be served at the same time. In general, this is the rule for multiple convictions stemming from the same event. But the judge always has discretion.

Under the previous system, individuals convicted of multiple murders served their life imprisonment sentences concurrently. Therefore, they were only subjected to one parole ineligibility period.

Families of victims in Canada have long argued that because life sentences for multiple murderers were served concurrently, it devalued each individual victim's life. Additionally, they argued that it put Canadians at risk by allowing multiple murderers to be paroled earlier than deserved. New legislation was enacted to ensure that individuals convicted of multiple murders serve a longer sentence before they are eligible for parole.

This type of sentencing is quite different from the U.S. system.

We sometimes hear that a U.S. judge has imposed several consecutive prison sentences on a criminal, adding up to more than 100 years. **Consecutive sentences are served one after the other**. In Canada, the Criminal Code states that sentences for crimes committed on different occasions can be ordered to be served consecutively. It is far less common to hear of sentences that long, but the Canadian system can still ensure some offenders will never get out of prison. The Criminal Code also states that offenses from the same incident should be served concurrently. A judge cannot sentence a person to more than one life sentence. Life is life. He will serve one life sentence, no matter what. However, because of concurrent sentencing, life imprisonment doesn't necessarily mean life in Canada.

For the most heinous and violent criminals, it should, though. A murder while committing sexual assault, hostage-taking, or terrorist activity is already deemed a first-degree murder punishable with life without parole eligibility for 25 years. Again, the same sentence applies if such a murder involves planning and deliberation.

Second-degree murder also carries a mandatory sentence of life imprisonment, but with a parole ineligibility period of between 10 years and 25 years, at the judge's discretion. Courts will determine the parole ineligibility period based on the gravity of the offense.

Contrary to common belief, public safety plays a lesser role, given the fact that the offender will be subject to a life sentence, and the Parole Board of Canada will presumably assess the present danger posed by the offender at the time of a parole application.

Now here comes the critical rule as it applies to the Shearing conviction for the murders of the Johnson and Bentley families. When an offender is convicted of multiple murders (either first or second-degree murder), the court can impose consecutive periods of parole ineligibility for each murder. These provisions of the Criminal Code came into force in December 2011 and permit a trial judge to impose consecutive parole ineligibility periods extending beyond 25 years after considering any jury recommendations. In the most extreme cases, this can result in a de facto term of life imprisonment without parole (i.e., a total parole ineligibility period extending beyond the offender's life expectancy.)

On December 2, 2011, the Protecting Canadians by Ending Multiple Murders Act was enacted. This Act ensures that individuals convicted of committing multiple murders serve their parole ineligibility period consecutively. This means the number of years allocated by a judge to be served without parole is now served one after another, not concurrently. Furthermore, judges are now able to impose consecutive 25-year parole ineligibility periods. The government's rationale is to allow one period of parole ineligibility for each victim. This applies to either first or second-degree murder convictions.

However, under this new legislation, it is not mandatory for a judge to impose consecutive parole ineligibility periods for offenders convicted of multiple murders. The judge maintains discretion in these cases. They may consider: the character of the offender, nature, and circumstances of the offense and any jury recommendations before deciding on whether to impose consecutive 25-year parole ineligibility periods.

To be sensitive to families and loved ones of victims, judges must state in writing or orally the basis for their decision to either impose or not impose consecutive parole ineligibility periods for offenders convicted of multiple murders.

Under the previous system, individuals convicted of multiple murders served their time concurrently. This meant they were eligible to apply for parole after serving just one period ranging from 10 to 25 years, depending on their sentence. For example, Clifford Olson killed eleven children but was eligible for parole after serving 25 years of his first-degree murder sentence.

There is no guarantee that parole will be granted to an offender. If the Parole Board of Canada determines that an offender still poses a risk to society, that person may be detained in prison past the parole eligibility period.

Any person released on parole from a term of life imprisonment or an indeterminate term of imprisonment must remain on parole, with conditions by the Parole Board, and are subject to electronic tagging for the remainder of their natural lives.

PAROLE BOARD OF CANADA

The Parole Board of Canada (PBC) is an independent administrative tribunal that makes release decisions, record suspension decisions (formerly pardons), and clemency recommendations regarding Canada's criminals. While independent, it is still part of the Canadian criminal justice system. The PBC "contributes to the protection of society by facilitating, as appropriate, the timely reintegration of offenders as law-abiding citizens. Public safety is the primary consideration in all PBC decisions."

Rules of the Parole Board in Canada

Victims wishing to receive information must first register with either the Parole Board of Canada (PBC) or the Correctional Service of Canada (CSC) – known as a victim notification request. They will then receive information about the offender for as long as they are under the PBC's jurisdiction, or until they ask to no longer be notified. Once a victim has registered with the PBC to receive information, they will receive

- The offender's name
- The offense and the court of conviction
- The sentence start date and length
- The offender's eligibility and review dates for unescorted temporary absences, parole, or statutory release

and can receive

- The offender's age
- The location of the penitentiary
- The date of any release on an unescorted temporary absence, or escorted temporary absence where the Board has approved the absence, parole, or statutory release
- The date of any Parole Board hearing
- Any conditions attached to an unescorted

temporary absence, parole, or statutory release
- The reason for an unescorted temporary absence
- The reason why an offender waived a hearing if one was given
- The destination of the offender when released on an unescorted temporary absence, parole, or statutory release, and if the offender will be in the vicinity of the victim while traveling to that destination
- Whether the offender is in custody and, if not, the reason
- Whether the offender has appealed a Board decision and the outcome of the appeal

What happens at a Parole Board Hearing?

A victim may attend the Parole Board of Canada (PBC) parole hearing of the offender who harmed them as an observer. Hearings typically take place inside the penitentiary where the offender is held.

A hearing is a face-to-face meeting between Board members and the offender. Its purpose is to help Board members assess the risk that an offender may pose should they be granted conditional release, and if this risk can be managed in the community. PBC hearings typically proceed like this

1. The offender, parole officer, RCO, victim(s), and observers are guided into the hearing room.
2. The Hearing Officer reads the procedural safeguards and asks the offender if their rights in the process have been followed.
3. If a victim has chosen to read a victim statement at the hearing, Board members will invite them to read their statement at some point before coming to a decision.
4. Board members ask the parole officer questions about the offender.
5. If the offender has an assistant, the assistant may make a statement to the Board members.
6. Board members ask the offender questions.
7. So, they may deliberate, Board members ask the offender, parole officer, observer, RCO, and victims to leave the hearing room. The RCO, victim, and observers wait in a separate area.
8. Board members discuss the offender's file information and analyze what they heard and decide.

9. The RCO escorts victims and observers back into the hearing room.
10. Board members state their decision and reasons. If the offender is granted parole, Board members state any special conditions the offender must follow and the reasons for those conditions.
11. Victims and observers are escorted from the hearing room by the RCO.

Under the Corrections and Conditional Release Act, only an offender can appeal a parole decision by the Parole Board of Canada (PBC).

A Victim's Statement

A victim may present a statement to PBC Board members at the offender's parole hearing that outlines the continuing impact the offense has had on them. As well, they may present any risk or safety concerns they feel the offender may pose.

Board Members

The PBC decision-makers are full-time or part-time members. They are Governor in Council (GIC) appointees made by the Governor-General of Canada, on the advice of the Queen's Privy Council of Canada (i.e., the Cabinet).

There are not more than 60 full-time members and a number of part-time members who hold office during good behavior, who are typically appointed for mandates of three to five years. There is a possibility of reappointment; however, there is no guarantee.

Preparation for hearings

Board members must examine many cases each day and render decisions crucial to public safety. Time management is an especially important skill, as each case can consist of several volumes of files. The content of the files can be very descriptive and disturbing.

Board members work independently, with little administrative support. Board members should be proficient in computer skills, especially in word processing.

In general, a Board member's workweek consists of two days of preparation for hearings, two days of hearings, and one day of in-office decisions.

On average, Board members must prepare three to six cases per hearing day. Each Board member must be thoroughly familiar with all files. Therefore, they should expect to spend at least six to eight hours reading and preparing for each hearing day. In some cases, preparation might take longer.

In addition to the established workload, Board members must further their knowledge and keep abreast of changes in decision-making and administrative policies on risk assessment.

Decision-Making: Hearings and Office Reviews

While the majority of the Board member's work is performed in the office, some of the work takes place in institutions. In some institutions (minimum and medium security), the Board members will be in the presence of offenders while walking the corridors.

The decisions are made by way of a hearing or in-office file review, by one or two Board members. Some hearings are also held by way of videoconference. Hearing days begin at 8:00 a.m. and rarely end before 4:30 p.m. All decisions are made the same day by the Board members and are rendered orally and in writing.

Hearings are conducted in close proximity to offenders. At times, Board members must be able to manage confrontational and aggressive behaviors. Some hearings are held in the presence of Indigenous Elders in accordance with Indigenous culture and spirituality. In some cases, the Elder performs a smudging ceremony by burning sacred herbs in the hearing room. Hearings can also be held in the presence of victims, offender assistants, observers, and journalists.

In general, Board members render eight in-office decisions on days intended for this purpose. Some Board members may also render decisions in record suspension cases.

Board members are often confronted by human misery. Board members must remain objective while being exposed to disturbing and offensive information.

They are to understand and apply Court decisions.

They are to work with another Board member to conduct hearings but render decisions independently.

Board members are to consider the protection of society as the main focus of decision-making.

They adopt well-developed interviewing skills and display active listening skills.

They are tasked with writing clear, concise, and comprehensive decisions based on a thorough risk assessment. These decisions should be able to withstand scrutiny from offenders, victims, and society in general."

PART III

TRIBUTE

JOHNSON BENTLEY AQUATIC CENTRE

| Johnson Bentley Aquatic Centre

The Johnson and Bentley memorial 25th-anniversary event was held on Saturday, October 19, 2013. The center has not only become a great dedication to the family. It has become something to remember the losses the family had, and a place to help realize what the people living here now have to appreciate in their lives.

It's become so important to the community, Ron Gorman, who owns the Gorman Brothers Lumber, donates $2,500 every year to the aquatic center, which gives to children that can't afford swimming lessons.

Louise Guarino, the administrator for the center since it opened, said, "It's just an incredible thing to see. My own kids grew up here, and I have grandchildren running around here somewhere. I tell people all the time that I work in the best place in the world. This is home, and my kids home, I'm really truly blessed."

All too often, the members of the victim's families and friends never get to meet the police or detectives that work on solving a case, other than as just a name in a police report or on the local news. So, when now-retired constable Ron German heard about a ceremony that was being held for the members of the Johnson and Bentley families, he knew that he had to go. "I was looking forward to showing my support." German said. "I was also looking forward to meeting all of the people who lost loved ones and were affected by the murders. I didn't know what I would say when we met, but from the time we met, we instantly bonded."

What surprised me the most was what German told me next, "When I was introduced to the families, it was Art Johnson, Bob Johnson's brother, who I soon found out had been waiting (at the time) almost 30 years, to hear the first-hand details on my contact with Shearing." I think in order for ordinary people to become closer to the police, we need to be fully involved in each other's lives. This waiting for information should not happen, especially when both sides want to get together and talk about the crime.

The murders took a heavy toll on Art Johnson over the years. But as German explains, you would never have known it by his charming and calm personality. I think that it is especially important for the police officers that work on a murder case like this one that they make a connection with the surviving family members. This meeting had become particularly important as German said, "I soon realized that meeting everyone filled in a missing piece for the family, something that was important to them, and it was also very important to me. When I got into police work, I had the idealistic goal to be there to help people in times of need. Although there is a lot of tough slogging for every success and you never see the fruits of your efforts. This made it very gratifying for me that our meeting and friendship has helped everyone, including myself, deal with the tragedy, just by being friends."

50TH WEDDING ANNIVERSARY

"Godfrey and Jennie Johnson would like to thank everyone for all the lovely cards, gifts, flowers, and all the help in honoring their 50th wedding anniversary." This is what the letter said that went out to all of the attendees of the open house that was held at Bob and Jackie Johnson's West Kelowna house on Saturday, November 7, 1981. The 110 attendees came from different parts of Canada, including Saskatchewan, Kamloops, and Tsawwassen.

The celebration took place in Godfrey and Jennie's home, located in West Kelowna, where they had lived in the basement of the home. The upstairs they shared with Bob and Jackie Johnson, with their two daughters, Janet and Karen.

It was a real family affair, with Bob's brother,

Art, and his wife, Bernice Johnson. Along with their children, Brian, and Sharlene, who recently had a new-born, Kristal, with her husband, Tom. Bob's twin sister, Elaine, along with her husband Russell Woods, also came with their two children Shelley and Rodney. The party wouldn't be complete without Bob's Boss and friend for over 20 years, Ron Gorman, who showed up smiling and beer on hand.

With all of the excitement of everyone getting together, nobody could possibly have thought that it would be the last time, for, in less than one year, a family would leave for a holiday and never return. The laughter, talking, and sound of beer bottle caps being opened drifted throughout the sunny but cool day. Though it was November, the region still had not had its first freeze, and in fact, most days were still pretty mild, around 50 F. Guests not only filled the house but were sitting around the backyard. After all, this is Canada, home of people wearing shorts right through the winter.

West Kelowna, as it's known now, was called Westbank in 1981, though it was part of the Okanagan, and only a bridge across a lake away from the Kelowna, the largest city in the interior of British Columbia, it had its very own identity.

JANET & KAREN JOHNSON

Janet, at her friends (She didn't want me to use her name in the book because she is so scared of Shearing being released and coming after her) birthday party - 1980 West Kelowna, B.C., on the lower left of picture wearing her red jacket. Karen was there too, but she was hiding during the picture taking as she was very shy.

Karen joined the West Bank Elementary Basketball Club for the 1981-82 Season and is in the bottom row, second to the right wearing a plaid shirt.

Karen joined the Guitar Club for the 1981-82 season and is in the top row on the right wearing plaid.

TO GET OUR TREE - KAREN JOHNSON

He always climbs up it and looks down for he says you can't tell if it is good by looking up. Anyway, when we decorate the tree we always put our decorations that we made in kindergarten. My mom and dad always let Janet and I get to open presents on Christmas Eve and look what Santa brought us and see what we got in our stocking. And Christmas day we get up open our presents that are under the tree then we go to my Aunties for supper. Christmas sure is fun!

23

THE UNBELIEVABLE SWEDE BY JACKIE JOHNSON

| Jackie & Janet Johnson

This was a letter that Jackie Johnson wrote about her husband Bob Johnson, which came across to me as the most honest, loving, and real thing I had heard about Bob from so many other people that knew him.

> *His name is Bob and his age is thirty-six*
> *And he likes to be in the hills and the sticks.*
>
> *Sweden is the country his family is from*
> *Smorgasbord and whiskey is tradition by crumb.*
>
> *At an early age one thing he was taught*
> *To swallow whole fish without getting caught.*
>
> *He's tried a lot of things in his own time*
> *But I'm proud of the fact that he is mine.*
>
> *A farmer he said he wanted to be*
> *Until he found how much work to a tree.*
>
> *He wanted his orchard with ditch*

irrigation
But I did the changing, a constant irritation.

The pruning, the thinning, the picking to do
Too much for the one man when working out too.

His hair is light brown and his eyes are blue
One of his interests is Bruce Lee and Kung Fu.

People are welcome from far and near
And they are greeted with an icy cold beer.

Tools he brings home bag after bag
If I bring up the subject I'm called a nag

He's a very proud father and loves his small girls
With their rosy cheeks and bouncy curls.

They both agree that he's really grand

As he fixes their toys with a loving hand.

Gorman's sawmill is his pride and joy
Started 18 years, when he was a boy.

He'll bust his butt for a thousand board feet
To hold onto his record that can't be beat.

He likes to Ski-doo and take to the hills
He goes like the devil with not many spills.

Summer will find him out in a boat
A few fish, a few beers, while keeping afloat.

He can laugh at most things and not get mad
Which makes his family very happy, not sad?

But some of the things we don't find so funny

*If you have the time I'll tell you a
  honey.*

*He spent all of our savings on a funny
  small car*
*It was supposed to go everywhere but
  didn't go far.*

*Peerless and Thompson, he bought
  what they had*
If you ask me, he simply went mad.

*He brought home screws, washers,
  iron, and wire,*
Nuts and bolts and even a tire.

Bag after bag, I can't mention them all
*They cluttered the basement wall to
  wall.*

We all agree he's a funny little guy
*But we wouldn't trade him, we
  wouldn't even try.*

*For we all think he's the pick of the
  bunch*
*He'll really come through when were
  in a crunch.*

24

JOHN GORMAN 65TH BIRTHDAY LETTER BY BOB JOHNSON

Bob & Janet Johnson

"Bob Johnson worked for the Gorman Bros. Lumber," Ross Gorman remembered. "He was never late, and he never missed a day's work. The community was in shock to think that something like this could happen. This man, Shearing, he has a warped mind, and he could never be trusted again. I hope the parole board sees fit to keep him locked up forever."

This letter was written on June 10, 1982, less than two months before Bob Johnson's death:

Dear John Gorman

Happy 65th birthday, John.

When I first started to work for you at the sawmill in 1957, I often wondered how old you were. It took me 25 years to find out, but now I know. You were 40 years young, and I was 19 years old. That made you more than twice as old as me. Now I am 44, and you are 65, which puts you at one-third older than myself. It seems I am getting older twice as fast as you are!

As I look back over the 25 years I have been with the company, I have seen a lot of changes. It is hard to believe that the little sawmill I started at has developed into the size of plant it is today. Looking back on some old pictures of the mill in 1956-, it is hard to realize that even the site the mill is on now is still the same place it was back then as it has changed drastically. We used to be in just such a small hole with swamps and bullrushes around us.

I can remember back around 1960-61, I was offered a job as a spare sawyer at Troutman Garaway Sawmill in Peachland by their superintendent, Art Copp. He offered me twice the hourly wage, which I was working for at the time, but I turned it down. One of the reasons for turning it down was in appreciation you showed and loyalty that I felt for you and Ross and the faith you showed in me. As I look back, that was one of the wisest decisions I have ever made. I also was your full-time sawyer and not a spare.

It is hard to believe of all the small sawmills, and box plants we had around Westbank, Peachland, Summerland, and Kelowna in the 1950s and 60s are now all gone. Most of them bigger than your little sawmill and box plant at the time. Now here you are, still expanding and going strong. I can only believe it's through your good management, foresight, and the faith the employees had in you, Ross, and the company.

In all the years I have been with you and the company, I have never lost a day's pay through layoff. When things got a little slack back when I first started, you either kept me doing something in the mill or box plant which wasn't at all productive or profitable, or you and Ross gave me a job in your orchards pruning, hoeing around the trees, picking the fruit, rocks, etc. I'd do anything. Even after the big fire in November 1969, when the mill burnt down, you never laid me off. I was very thankful for that. I also feel that this might be some kind of record to work 25 years for a company and never to have been laid off.

I am also very thankful that you gave me the opportunity to learn to saw. It was you and Bill Wetton that taught me the basics of sawing. I remember you and Bill telling me, "the most important rule was to get the most lumber and the best quality out of your log. Production would come later with practice," you said. A slab at that time was all the waste with no chipper, so slabbing was very important.

I spent a summer canting logs on the carriage for you when you were sawing, and I would watch how you sawed the logs up. When a salesman or perspective lumber buyer came along, and you were busy talking to him, I would try cutting a few logs myself. That is how I got started sawing. Of all the jobs in the sawmill, planer, box plant, and bin plant I have done in the past, I still like sawing the best.

Talking to other employees working at other sawmills and plants and telling me of all their labor problems and strikes and the poor relationship between the workers and management, I strongly believe we have a very unique mill where the management and staff and employees get along so well. I consider myself very lucky to be working in an outfit like this. I know I'm speaking for most of all your employees here when I express my feelings about this.

John, now that you are 65 and will be getting

on the government payroll, I sincerely hope that you continue to be an active member of the company as you have always been. The kind of progress and expansion that you and Ross have done with this little old sawmill in the years that I have seen is really outstanding. I can only say that I am proud that I could be a part of the Gorman Bros. Company. The wages I have earned here have enabled me to have a family and to support them in a standard of living that has made us happy and secure, and on behalf of them, I also thank you.

Again, I wish you a very Happy 65th birthday and the very best in the future.
God bless you and yours

Yours sincerely,
Bob Johnson

AFTERWORD
SHELLEY BODEN, FAMILY MEMBER

For George & Edith Bentley, Bob, Jackie, Janet & Karen Johnson

---

When I was 18-years old, I was in the middle of a Grade 12 class when I was called to the principal's office. There I was informed of the horror and pain that had happened to my family. The summer of 1982 was like the plot of a horror movie. I used to love watching horror movies, but that was before I knew about the terrible, perverted things that a monster named David Shearing did to my family and especially my little cousins that night in Wells Gray Park.

Now, all I can think of when I see a horror film are the cruel, ugly things that happened to six members of my family. The vilest part is that David took it upon himself to savagely brutalize two children for sex. The girls never knew physical intimacy except for brutal, forced sexual assault by a deviant molester and murderer. Being abused by the man who killed your family is a horror I cannot imagine. He took it upon himself to end the lives of a whole family and shatter the lives of all their relatives and loved ones. As a woman and a mother, I am sickened beyond words that my cousin Janet's first kiss was from a monster in front of her terrified 11-year-old sister.

David not only created fear for my family, but he has frightened many other people in the communities of Clearwater, West Kelowna, and beyond. We feel the fear of being stalked, attacked without warning, and murdered without mercy. We feel the fear of young girls being abused and murdered by an evil man, just as what happened to Janet and Karen. It still has not been made known what he did to those girls during those horrible days they were alive and scared. What's the truth? Now our family has to tell the little children among us that monsters are real. If David is truly remorseful, he will tell us what really happened and stop applying for parole. If David Shearing/Ennis is released under any circumstances, we fear for our lives, we fear for the safety of others, and we fear he will re-offend if given a chance. He will never deserve that chance.

— SHELLEY BODEN, SEPTEMBER 2020

ACKNOWLEDGMENTS

LAW ENFORCEMENT

I want to express my appreciation to all law enforcement people involved in this case. It is only because of your hard work and dedication to helping the victims and their families that resulted in catching, convicting, and sending the killer to prison. I recognize not only the long hours and detailed policing that you all have done, but also the emotional toll that this case must have had on all of you. I realize that when you take on a murder case and are exposed to all of the evidence like forensics, photos, and learning the horror of what some people do to others, while trying to live your own lives with your family, children, and friends, the strain must be almost unbearable.

A special thanks to retired RCMP Sgt. Mike Eastham and his book *The Seventh Shadow,* a great explanation and reference of how a group of great men worked such a horrendous case as this one. The details of what is necessary to discover missing people, recover their bodies, scientifically detail what happened, arrest, and bring the culprit to trial. All while trying to live their own lives without revealing even a hint of the anguish and pain they go through is incredible.

Eastham had to handle several of his own personal issues during this time. Including a separation from his wife, legal battles over a bar he once owned, and a supervisor that did everything he could to make this investigation harder than it had to be, just because he didn't like him. Eastham made many sacrifices to get the results needed in this case and bring the culprit to justice. Eastham's book is a must-read for anyone interested in the details of what law enforcement deal with while working a murder case.

A special thanks to retired RCMP Constable Ron German. He was always willing to put himself fully into the case to locate and help make sure that the perpetrator was caught, jailed, and convicted. After the trial was over, even though he had never met any of the victim's remaining friends and family, he still appeared at the memorial for the victims. And in his original uniform! (that in itself is amazing) Since then, it has become a regular event for him to visit with them every time he comes to the area. I found Ron always available for me to answer questions and have some great discussions about the things involved in true crime policing. German shows not only his outstanding dedication to his work but to the people he served while being a policeman.

During the finishing of this book, another vital officer that worked on this case had died. The following obituary is a special dedication to him, Sgt. Ken "Reliable" Leibel!

Henry Kenneth Leibel
Sergeant (Rtd)
Regimental #28611
1951 - 2020
Years of Service: 1971 - 1992
Postings: "E"

It is with great sadness that the family of Henry Kenneth Leibel announce his passing at the age of 68 on Easter Sunday, April 12, 2020 in Port Moody, BC.

Ken passed away peacefully with his wife Tanya and her daughter Maegan by his side after battling with frontal lobe dementia for several years.

Ken was born on December 18, 1951 in Qu'Appelle, Saskatchewan to Henry and Ethel Leibel. He spent his early years on the farm before enrolling in the RCMP at the age of 18. Ken was a proud and respected member of the RCMP having served his entire career in British Columbia.

His favourite pastime was to share stories about his challenges and successes, and a few years ago wrote his memoirs for the family, providing insight into his years of service. He also loved to play crib and would never turn down anyone who challenged him to a game - he loved to win! After the RCMP, he provided investigative services for ICBC and polygraph services for the federal government.

Ken was predeceased by his father Henry, brother Doug and sister Rhonda. He is survived by his wife Tanya, and her children Maegan (Chris Langridge, Adam and Ellie) and Adam Turnbull; stepchildren Michelle, Cory, Jason, Hollie, Shane and their families; mother Ethel, siblings Fred, Karen (Martin) Kuntz, Shannon and Shelly (Dino) Toniello; brother-in-law John Graham; and numerous nieces and nephews.

Ken will be laid to rest in Saskatchewan at a later date.

In lieu of flowers, donations in memory of Ken may be made to the Alzheimer Society or to Friends of the RCMP Heritage Centre.

THE FAMILY

There is a great sense of duty and obligation to the victims and their families in writing a book. I have a responsibility to each of the victims, their families, and friends to find and tell the truth. That also means listening and researching each of the stories heard during this process. I have an obligation to show proper respect for each of their lives because they deserve no less. The strength I found amongst the Johnson and Bentley families was extraordinary. I can't imagine what it would have been like to live through this trauma to my family and me in the early 1980s.

As far as the killer and what he said during this book's writing, I consumed it, and included what was needed to be read by the readers. This is not a book about his life as it stands now, which I think he would have wanted it to be – a pleading of his case to the reader about how he should be free now to finish living out his life with a wife and happiness. But it's not. This book is a story of a family trying to live and enjoy their lives when he decided to end them for his own selfish reasons. So, expect only to hear his words when needed. I refuse to showcase the bad choices he made and plead for his freedom and your forgiveness.

Dear Reader, as you read through this story,

imagine yourself being in the position of any member of these families and what you would do if you were in their place. And kindly remember that even after you have read their story and can empathize with such a tragedy, after you've finished the book, you get to put it away and go back to your own life. It is not much more than a bad nightmare for you. But for the family, it is and was their life. They were all expected to move forward, get married, and have children with this memory running through the back of their minds every day. Just think about after living that nightmare, one of your kids asking you if they could go camping? Or how it would feel any time one of your kids was late coming from school or work.

When I first found and approached the family members, I wasn't sure what kind of responses I'd receive. As an author, you get a lot of rejection, and I don't blame anyone who does reject an offer. It must be the last thing that anyone would want to do – relive something they've probably wanted to forget their whole life. But also as an author, there's nothing harder than listening to people's happy times in their lives through pictures and stories, knowing how it ends so tragically.

The Johnson and Bentley families were great! They were anxious to talk about the case and wanted me to know whatever I needed for the book. As you'll learn, the killer was caught and put in prison. He has applied for parole twice already, was denied, but it's coming up again in 2021. The trauma is ongoing for these families. How a heinous killer of six innocent people can actually be allowed to reenter mainstream society and live among us is unfathomable. Would you want him as your neighbor? There's also the chance of him getting free on day passes, which can be with or without guards.

A special thanks to Shelley Boden for getting her family together for us to talk, and thanks to Sharlene Johnson for all of her great information on the family.

REFERENCES

1. *Master Detective – Canada's Most Horrendous Crime,* Jack G. Heise, RGH Publishing, 1982
2. Tumbler Ridge News, November 13, 2013, Trent Ernst, Editor
3. Police Report, December 01, 1983, Johnson/Bentley Murders
4. Government of Canada Memorandum, 18 April, 1984, S.F. Thompson Supervisor Appreciation
5. Search Warrant for Shearing house & cabin, November 20th 1983
6. Occurrence Report, November 16, 1983, Tumbler Ridge Interrogation Report
7. Undertaking to Appear Document - David Shearing, Tumbler Ridge RCMP
8. Parole Hearing Report, June 30, 2012
9. Calgary Sun, July 2, 2008, Michael Platt, "Wife of convicted Killer says she forgives him"
10. Calgary Sun, July 1, 2008, Michael Platt, "He killed six people, including two kids he sexually abused and now David William Shearing wants out of prison"

11. Alberta Law Report, December 12, 1983
12. www.680news, September 18, 2012, News Staff, "B.C. Mass murderer David Shearing says sorry, but still denied parole"
13. CBC News, December 13, 2000, "Murderers wife unfairly fired"
14. *The Seventh Shadow,* RCMP SGT. Michael Eastham (ret.), 1999, ISBN 1-894020-47-2, Warwick Publishing
15. https://www.cbc.ca/news/canada/cbc-explains-sentences-concurrent-consecutive-1.5005853
16. https://crcvc.ca/docs/consecutive-sentencing-2012.pdf
17. https://laws-lois.justice.gc.ca/eng/acts/C-46/section-231.html
18. https://www.cbc.ca/news/canada/calgary/consecutive-murder-convictions-1.5144202
19. CBC News, September 11, 2013, "Travis Baumgartner gets 40 years without parole for killing co-workers"
20. nationalpost.com, April 25, 2013, "Harper government supports private bill that could bring minimum 40-year sentences for some violent crimes"
21. Globe & Mail, May 6, 2014, Sean Fine,

"Five fundamental ways Harper has changed the justice system"
22. Benjamin Perrin is a law professor at UBC and senior fellow at the Macdonald-Laurier Institute, which is publishing his latest paper analyzing the Life Means Life Act (macdonaldlaurier.ca).
23. https://www.shrinktank.com/women-marry-prisoners/august2019
24. https://www.iol.co.za/news/opinion/meet-the-women-who-marry-prisoners-1786269
25. https://thoughtcatalog.com/jim-goad/2018/06/prison-brides-hybristophilia-and-women-who-fall-in-love-with-really-bad-boys/
26. http://www.drlaurablog.com/2012/01/18/women-who-love-prisoners/
27. https://www.thestar.com/news/canada/2016/10/30/conjugal-visits-help-canadian-inmates-reintegrate-into-society-experts-say.html
28. https://www.theglobeandmail.com/news/national/jailhouse-weddings-questioned/article18283404/
29. Appavoo, D. (1995). *Evaluative Study of Inmate Marriages in the Federal Institutions.... and Guidelines for CSC*

Chaplaincy Involvement. Unpublished manuscript

30. *HOW TO MARRY AN INMATE IN CANADA* The data collection, using interviews and a semi-structured questionnaire, and an initial report were completed under contract by David Appavoo (Appavoo, 1995).
31. https://www.psychologytoday.com/us/blog/the-new-brain/201610/humans-are-genetically-predisposed-kill-each-other
32. R. Douglas Fields, *"Why We Snap"* p. 286, 2016.
33. Delta Optimist, November 15, 2008, Jessica Kerr
34. Vancouver Sun, November 8, 2008, Larissa Liepens, "Women who love killers"
35. Daily Courier, Ron Seymour, 2008, "Killer coming up for Parole"
36. Vancouver Sun, October 23, 2008, Jamie Komarnicki and Elise Stolte
37. Kamloops Daily Courier, October 18, 2008, Susan Duncan, "Their lives ended Right Here"
38. https://www.health.harvard.edu/newsletter_article/pessimism-about-pedophilia

39. https://www.vice.com/en_us/article/mbzj5q/pedophiles-cant-be-cured-and-its-dangerous-to-suggest-they-can
40. https://www.routledgehandbooks.com/doi/10.4324/9781315716596.ch28
41. https://nationalpost.com/news/canada/ottawa-clinic-says-it-can-cure-pedophilia-but-critics-argue-the-claim-is-unproven-and-dangerous
42. https://www.psychotherapy.org.uk/reflections-ex-paedophile-cured-nhs-psychoanalytic-psychotherapy/

ABOUT THE AUTHOR

Alan R. Warren has written several Best-Selling True Crime books and has been one of the hosts and producer of the popular NBC news talk radio show *House of Mystery* which reviews True Crime, History, Science, Religion, Paranormal mysteries that we live with  every day. From a darker, comedic and logical perspective, he has interviewed guests such as Robert Kennedy Jr., F. Lee Bailey, Aphrodite Jones, Marcia Clark, Nancy Grace, Dan Abrams and Jesse Ventura. The show is based in Seattle on KKNW 1150 AM and syndicated on the NBC network throughout the United States including on KCAA 106.5 FM Los Angeles/Riverside/Palm Springs, as well in Utah, New Mexico, and Arizona.

www.alanrwarren.com

ALSO BY ALAN R. WARREN

BEYOND SUSPICION: RUSSELL WILLIAMS — A CANADIAN SERIAL KILLER

Young girl's panties started to go missing; sexual assaults began to occur, and then female bodies were found! Soon this quiet town of Tweed, Ontario, was in a panic. What is even more shocking was when an upstanding resident stood accused of the assaults. This was not just any man, but a pillar of the community; a decorated military pilot who had flown Canadian Forces VIP aircraft for dignitaries such as the Queen of England, Prince Philip, the Governor-General and Prime Minister of Canada.

This is the story of serial killer Russell Williams, the elite pilot of Canada's Air Force One, and the innocent victims he murdered. Unlike other serial killers, Williams seemed very unaffected about his crimes and leading two different lives.

Alan R. Warren describes the secret life including the abductions, rape, and murders that were unleashed on an unsuspecting community. Included are letters written to the victims by Williams and descriptions of the assaults and rapes as seen on videos and photos taken by Williams during the attacks.

This updated version also contains the full brilliant police interrogation of Williams and his confession. Also, the twisted way the Williams planned to pin his crimes on his unsuspecting neighbor.

DOOMSDAY CULTS: THE DEVIL'S HOSTAGES

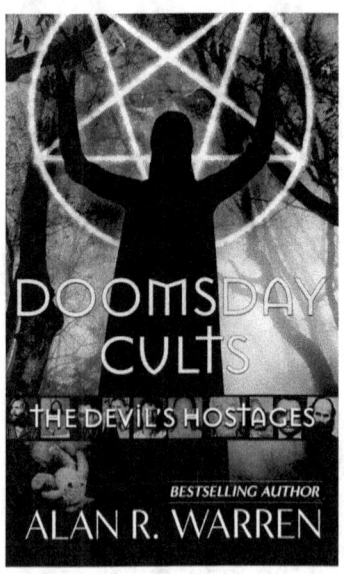

Jim Jones convinced his 1000 followers they would all have to commit suicide since he was going to die. Shoko Asahara convinced his followers to release a weapon of mass destruction, the deadly sarin gas, on a Tokyo subway. The Order of the Solar Temple lured the rich and famous, including Princess Grace of Monaco, and convinced them to die a fiery death now on Earth to be reborn on a better planet called Sirius. Charles Manson convinced his followers to kill, in an attempt to incite an apocalyptic race war.

These are a few of the doomsday cults examined in this book by bestselling author Alan R. Warren. Its focus is on cults whose destructive behavior was due in large part to their apocalyptic beliefs or doomsday movements. It includes details surrounding the massacres and a look into how their members became so brainwashed they committed unimaginable crimes at the command of their leader.

Usually, when we hear about these cults and their massacres, we ask ourselves how it possibly happened. We could also ask ourselves, what then is the difference between a cult and a religion? We once had a small group of people who unquestionably followed a person who believed he was the son of God. Two thousand years later, that following is one of the most recognized religions in the world. This book in no way criticizes believing in God. Rather, it examines how a social movement grows into a full religion and when it does not. And what makes the conventional faiths such as Christianity, Judaism, Islam, and Hinduism stand above groups such as the Branch Davidians or Children of God.

IN CHAINS: THE DANGEROUS WORLD OF HUMAN TRAFFICKING

Human trafficking is the trade of people for forced labor or sex. It also includes the illegal extraction of human organs and tissues. And it is an extremely ruthless and dangerous industry plaguing our world today.

Most believe human trafficking occurs in countries with no human rights legislation. This is a myth. All types of human trafficking are alive and well in most of the developed countries of the world like the United States,

Canada, and the UK. It is estimated that $150 billion a year is generated in the forced labor industry alone. It is also believed that 21 million people are trapped in modern-day slavery – exploited for sex, labor, or organs.

Most also believe since they live in a free country, there is built-in protection against such illegal practices. But for many, this is not the case. Traffickers tend to focus on the most vulnerable in our society, but trafficking can happen to anyone. You will see how easy it can happen in the stories included in "In Chains."

WARNING This book contains graphic details and statements that some may find very disturbing.

www.ingramcontent.com/pod-product-compliance
Lightning Source LLC
Chambersburg PA
CBHW071954070526
44583CB00015B/1191